LEGAL AND FINANCIAL ASPECTS OF ARCHITECTURAL CONSERVATION

Smolenice Castle (Marc Denhez)

LEGAL AND FINANCIAL ASPECTS OF ARCHITECTURAL CONSERVATION

The Smolenice Castle Conference Central Europe

edited by
Marc Denhez
Stephen Neal Dennis

Dundurn Press
Toronto • Oxford

Editor: Wendy Thomas
Designers: Sebastian Vasile and Barry Jowett
Printer: Webcom

Canadian Cataloguing in Publication Data

Main entry under title:
    Legal and financial aspects of architectural conservation

Essays arising from the Smolenice Castle Conference held at Smolenice Castle, Slovakia, November 1994.

Includes bibliographical references and index.

ISBN 1-55002-250-4

1. Historic buildings — Law and legislation.   2. Historic buildings — Conservation and restoration.   3. Historic preservation — Law and legislation.   I. Denhez, Marc, 1949-   II. Dennis, Stephen N.   III. Smolenice Castle Conference (1994).

K3791.L43 1997   344'.094   C96–990024–4

1   2   3   4   5   BJ   01   00   99   98   97

THE CANADA COUNCIL | LE CONSEIL DES ARTS
FOR THE ARTS | DU CANADA
SINCE 1957 | DEPUIS 1957

We acknowledge the support of the **Canada Council for the Arts** for our publishing program. We also acknowledge the support of the **Ontario Arts Council** and the **Book Publishing Industry Development Program** of the **Department of Canadian Heritage.**

 Printed on recycled paper.

Dundurn Press
8 Market Street
Suite 200
Toronto, Ontario, Canada
M5E 1M6

Dundurn Press
73 Lime Walk
Headington, Oxford
England
OX3 7AD

Dundurn Press
250 Sonwil Drive
Buffalo, NY
U.S.A. 14225

TABLE OF CONTENTS

ACADEMIA ISTROPOLITANA BRATISLAVA
INSTITUTE OF ADVANCED STUDIES

ARCHITECTURAL AND URBAN HERITAGE CONSERVATION

International Conference on Legal and Financial Aspects of Architectural and Conservation in Central Europe
Smolenice Castle
Slovakia
November 6-9, 1994

October 28, 1994

I am pleased to welcome all the outstanding experts and participants from different countries that have joined our international conference in Smolenice.

Lack of adequate preservation legislation is not only a Slovak problem but a current problem in the whole of Central Europe. Therefore, we are pleased that our invitation to attend this conference was accepted by domestic and foreign representatives.

Our endeavours to draw attention to preservation legislation were supported by a grant from the International Research & Exchanges Board in the United States and the Pro Slovakia state cultural fund, as well as several additional foundations. We are very grateful for the financial support, as well as for the moral support shown by the presence of several outstanding experts who accepted our invitations to present papers at this conference. At this time I would especially like to thank Mr. Stephen Neal Dennis for his help in preparing this conference.

I hope that this conference will fill the gap in the dissemination of preservation legislation information and bring to all of you new impetus for your work.

Sincerely,

Alena Brunovska
Director of AI

Embassy of the United States of America

Bratislava, Slovak Republic
October 31, 1994

International Conference on Historic Preservation Legislation
Smolenice Castle
Smolenice
Slovak Republic

As the United States Ambassador to the Slovak Republic, I am pleased to send greetings to all the participants in the International Conference on Historic Preservation Legislation. A wealth of monuments and masterpieces testifies to the rich cultural heritage of Slovakia and Central Europe, despite the ravages of war, neglect, and totalitarian demolition. This heritage must be preserved through legislation and the efforts of concerned citizens.

I am delighted to note the American role in this conference. The six American presenters are leading experts in preservation law. By comparing European and North American approaches to historical preservation, conferees will gain valuable insights and perspectives. I am also pleased that funds for this conference have been provided by American NGOs, IREX and the Kress Foundation.

In closing I want to thank the Academia Istropolitana for organizing this event and wish all of you an enjoyable and informative conference.

Sincerely,

Theodore E. Russell
American Ambassador

Acknowledgements

Co-operating Co-sponsoring Organizations
Academia Istropolitana (Bratislava, Slovakia)
US/ICOMOS (Washington, D.C.)

CONFERENCE ORGANIZERS
Jaroslav Kilián, Academia Istropolitana, Bratislava
Stephen Neal Dennis, Washington, D.C.

EDITORS
Marc Denhez, Ottawa (Rapporteur)
Stephen Neal Dennis, Washington, D.C.

TRANSLATION
From Slovak: Elizabeth Yenchko-Facinelli
From Russian: Arkady Salamancha

The preparation of this conference and this report was supported by a grant from the **INTERNATIONAL RESEARCH & EXCHANGES BOARD (IREX),** with funds provided by the U.S. Department of State (Title VIII), and the **JOHN D. AND CATHERINE MacARTHUR FOUNDATION.** Additional funding to assist with the organization of the conference was provided by the **SAMUEL KRESS FOUNDATION**, the **COUNCIL OF EUROPE** and the **STATE CULTURAL FOUNDATION PRO SLOVAKIA.** Preliminary support was also provided through the **NATIONAL CENTRE FOR PRESERVATION LAW**, Washington, D.C. Additional printed materials were made available courtesy of the **CANADIAN COMMISSION FOR UNESCO** and the **FEDERATION OF CANADIAN MUNICIPALITIES.**

None of these organizations, however, is responsible for the views expressed at the conference or in this report.

The integrally related Demonstration Sites Visit (November 9-11, 1994) to Vlkolínec, Levoča, Spiš and Banská Štiavnica was organized in co-operation with local units of the **INSTITUTE FOR MONUMENTS** (Slovakia) and key local officials.

/AJ

ACADEMIA ISTROPOLITANA BRATISLAVA
INSTITUTE OF ADVANCED STUDIES
ARCHITECTURAL AND URBAN HERITAGE CONSERVATION

International Conference on Legal and Financial Aspects of Architectural Conservation Smolenice Castle
Slovakia
November 6-9, 1994

Conference Theses

Actual context of cultural heritage conservation and rebuilding democratic societies in Central Europe.

Jaroslav Kilián

Property rights in the last period were violated in the name of the "public interest." It was possible, without any reasonable justification or compensation, to override individual and/or author group rights on property. The individual as well as the local community were not able to contradict or confront the State. Protection of cultural heritage represents a certain limitation of property rights. Protecting generally-declared national or universal cultural values is accompanied by a limitation of the owner's rights in dealing freely with land and buildings. Appropriate legislation can establish favourable conditions for mutual agreement.

Physical planning can be a very efficient tool to enable harmonious economic and environmental development. Urbanism, as a science, can analyze phenomena such as urban growth and set up tools to maintain the necessary control on the negative impact of spontaneous actions and behaviour of land users on society and the environment. Physical planning has to include cultural heritage as a strategic choice.

Building codes or laws controlling building activity establish basic equal rights and duties for those who want to use and develop their property in a relation to their neighbours and their community. Hygiene, security, fire safety, and general aesthetic criteria, among others, must be taken into consideration. On one hand, preservation of historic buildings and sites limits free use, but on the other, it is often in conflict with new standards. This demands a special approach.

The success or failure of the whole process of cultural heritage preservation depends on sensitive implementation of strategy and appropriate use of available tools. Awareness of predominant public values, and understanding of the cultural heritage as a part of individual identity, are the only way toward integrated preservation. Tolerance and respect of cultural diversity is one step in building a democratic society. Administration of public affairs has to be based on democratic principles. Legislation establishes guidelines for this.

Economic aspects of the preservation of cultural monuments are the fundamental basis for a realistic understanding of the complex problem. Legal protection of historic monuments has to include financial aspects from its inception. Compensation, positive stimulation and punishment have to be balanced in order to deal efficiently with ways to achieve cultural goals. It is not possible to resolve conservation problems with only the State's resources, as was proved during the long period of centrally-planned national economy, but financial tools (when sensitively applied) can be very effective in historic preservation.

Quality control and consumer protection are of high interest for our society. Dealing with historic materials demands special skill and ability. Irreversible damage can be caused to cultural property by non-professional action, and all social effort towards preservation can thus be devalued. Legislation can help create a reasonable system of control and limits.

Inventories and collections of other movable property are the subject of financial pressure related to the economic changes in Central Europe. The opening of and free movement throughout the former "iron Curtain" are creating a new market for antiquities. The rise of organized crime represents a serious problem in preserving objects of artistic and historic value in situ. It is obvious that most owners (particularly churches, small communities, and individuals due to changes in society) have other financial priorities that the protection of cultural property. Some technical solutions are too expensive and, with the lack of a system of safeguards, not very efficient. Legal action at the national and international level is indispensable.

Integrated natural and cultural landscape preservation is the object of new directions in the philosophy of conservation. The scale of such action creates specific problems. Education of professionals is an indispensable condition in developing structures for cultural heritage protection. Administrative, legal, scientific, and technical bodies in preservation need qualified people. The understanding of the dimensions of cultural heritage, by the public at large, is the sine qua non on the way towards real preservation strategy.

Background

IN 1993, ORGANIZATIONS IN Bratislava and Washington began joint efforts to convene a conference on national legislative strategy for the conservation of historic buildings. Such conferences are extremely rare internationally; in Central Europe, they were unprecedented.

Around the world, there have been major upheavals within the last decade: entire political, economic and administrative systems have been turned upside down. Many countries have been called upon to "re-invent" the entirety of the socio-economic context for their great architectural and historic symbols, and even in countries where the upheaval was less dramatic, international economic pressures have forced governments to explore more cost-efficient ways of dealing with older buildings, neighbourhoods and entire cities. Of all the regions where one can study the transition in socio-economic systems, the situation is particularly dramatic in Central Europe. In many respects, Slovakia represented an ideal venue in which to explore how countries can revisit their national strategies on the ongoing viability and prosperity of their older buildings and districts.

The feasibility of such a conference was discussed by the US committee of the International Council on Monuments and Sites (US/ICOMOS) and by the Academia Istropolitana, in the Slovak capital of Bratislava. This institution has offered a one-year certificate program since 1991 on Architectural and Urban Heritage Conservation, taught entirely in English. Visiting foreign faculty supplement presentations made by staff at the Academia Istropolitana, which was named for a distinguished institution that existed in Bratislava from 1465 until 1490.

In November 1994, the conference was held at Smolenice Castle, a facility now owned and operated by the Slovak Academy of Sciences. The use of this location was suggested to the Academia Istropolitana by the Slovak Ambassador to the United States, a former president of the Academy of Sciences. Previously a hunting lodge for a wealthy Hungarian family, Smolenice Castle provided meeting spaces in attractive surroundings on the slopes of the Lower Carpathian Mountains, an hour's drive from Bratislava.

Eleven countries were represented at the podium. American speakers described, among other things, the U.S.A.'s controls on the public sector, which are generally acknowledged to be among the most advanced of their kind in the world; the Americans also described various incentive programs, which are rivalled in their originality only by a handful of countries in Western Europe. Speakers from Western Europe, for their part, described a variety of tools for the protection of private property (both movable and immovable), from the perspective of a region that has some 1,500 years of legislative experience in the area.

There were, however, some American comparisons on what was nonetheless feasible within a country confined by an elaborate system of constitutionally-entrenched property rights and an equally elaborate division of powers between levels of government. These features are significant to regions such as Central Europe, where the constitutional status of property rights and the division of governmental powers are all being renegotiated at the present time. These presentations were followed by the Central European perspective, i.e., of countries that are revisiting the entirety of their legislative apparatus and preparing for new systems at a time when tourism (including visitation of the "national heritage" and of historic cities) has inadvertently become the largest earner of foreign exchange — at precisely the moment when the relevant governments have the least available cash with which to put "their best foot forward." The presenters described the resulting squeeze in which national heritage agencies were left and the various legislative processes that had been launched to respond to the situation.

The sessions at Smolenice Castle were followed by a Demonstration Sites Visit to certain key sites in Slovakia that exemplified the challenges and opportunities ahead. The three-day Demonstration Sites Visit was organized to show conference participants the three World Heritage Sites in Slovakia, and to generate additional discussion about conference topics among participants and presenters.

Some of the presentations reflected a vague uneasiness about the subject-matter. For certain participants, "conservation" was a principle that could extend to a large percentage of the building stock; to others, the subject-matter was confined to "monuments." This ambiguity is reflective of a tension that exists in the international heritage movement as a whole, but that this conference did not propose to resolve. The focus instead was on pragmatic approaches that would be valid regardless of the theoretical definitions used.

This book documents the national strategies and tactics discussed at the Smolenice Castle conference. As the international community advances in the World Decade of Cultural Development, it is hoped that this kind of international exchange of ideas will be of direct assistance to any country that seeks to equip itself with legislative strategies to meet the challenges facing its national heritage in the immediate future.

PART I:

Strategy and Planning

Law, Heritage and Democratic Society

Jaroslav Kilián*

Contents

The goal of this exercise is not to address theory: it is to engage in a practical exchange of experiences, i.e., a platform for discussion among people who are equally responsible for the care of cultural monuments, who have experience, and who have achieved good results.

Societal background

Central Europe includes countries that are going through profound societal changes. The preservation of cultural monuments, however, is not a new question. For many years, there has been discussion of the problems in the conservation of monuments and their protection from threats, degradation and destruction. The subject is complex.

Methodology

The following introduction explores a few questions, beginning with the development of a philosophy about how to restore, e.g., about the relationship of monuments to society and to the development of democracy.

I will also explore the question of the methods that can be used to get funding for the preservation of cultural monuments and (from the professional viewpoint) to deal with the legal and legislative aspects of cultural preservation.

Historical evolution

Interest in the conservation of historical monuments has a tradition dating back hundreds of years. This interest has retained many of the same motives throughout this long period of time, but the methods by which society has attempted to achieve these goals have changed repeatedly. From the romantic collectors of curiosities to the interest in exceptional architecture, society has come to a greater understanding of architecture as a whole.

* Jaroslav Kilián, architect, is Head of the Program in Architectural and Heritage Conservation (Academia Istropolitana, Bratislava), and Past President of ICOMOS-Slovakia.

Evolving geographic scope

As a further step in the understanding of architecture, professionals started to look at groups of monuments, and society is now interested in towns, settlements, cultural landscapes and the environment. This is a definite development during recent years that shows that the cultural heritage is something that presents a wider picture than artifacts of museum interest: in today's society, we discuss the problems of "cultural identity," and cultural monuments are objects with which a society can identify.

Beyond "artifacts"

Personal dimension

For today's person, a monument is part of his/her environment. It is a part of all of life's actions, i.e., how that person lives. The attitudes with which professionals view the conservation of monuments would not be well developed if this conservation were viewed only as a physical action, with no moral or spiritual overtones. There is, in the preservation of monuments, a relationship between a person and his/her culture and environment.

In this new era, Central Europe is being restructured as a democratic society. We are not building something entirely new: indeed for many years, this was the tradition in which our societies grew. There have been certain disturbances which interrupted this life:

Relation to social history

- from the viewpoint of personal lives these events were (and are) impossible to ignore,
- but from the viewpoint of the development of society as a whole, this was just one episode.

The conservation community, which has a positive relationship to cultural monuments, must be conscious of the fact that these values have a long life: compared to the qualities that are intrinsic to cultural heritage, the cycle of political change is much shorter and much less important.

Today's democratic society is being built on the foundation of basic human rights.

Keystone: The balancing of rights

Among human rights belong:

- property rights, and
- the right to a cultural identity.

Participation

Society must conduct itself with laws that guarantee that public actions will be decided with the participation of all those who create that society. There is no longer any toleration for authoritarian actions of the State over its citizens.

Role of law

Legal relationships and laws create a framework for this kind of behaviour. With respect to the preservation of monuments, one has to consider two basic issues.

- First is the public interest in protecting the cultural heritage that belongs to everyone, i.e., not just to the owner but to the entire society.
- On the other hand, society must ensure that the enabling factors that are used do not disrupt other laws.

Current
challenge

It is essential to minimize conflicts between the interest of the public and the interest of the individual. That is why it is necessary to look for tools that are non-adversarial for the preservation of monuments. In other words, the law for the preservation of monuments should work in a preventive way and in a positive way. As of today, however, we cannot say that conservation of monuments allows us to use any method to truly attain our goal. Other democratic societies are already following the methods that Central Europe is hoping to use and are achieving some success. Conservation goals are proving difficult to fulfil (by those who are responsible for the preservation of monuments); it is a question of the capability to negotiate, to discuss, to decide and to mediate between the public interest and the interest of the individual. This task must turn on professionalism.

Actions based
on standards,
not instincts

If the law of historic preservation is being changed, it is important to create a good context for the conservation of monuments. As long as the law is used to create possibilities for historic preservation work, it should also create possibilities to mediate the relationships with and among the owners. These laws must be implemented professionally and objectively: professionals cannot depend simply only on their own convictions (that they are acting in the public interest).

Reality check

What are the heritage community's goals in this respect? How does it define its priorities? There is a big difference between that which it would wish, and that which is realistic based on these complicated economic and societal relationships. The formulation of goals and methods — not just relating to financial arrangements, but relating to our capabilities, intellect and interpersonal relationships — must be based on real possibilities. In the past, these control mechanisms did not exist in Central Europe. The assessment of goals, realistically based on efforts by people, did not exist.

Objectivity

For many professionals, the cultural monument that they wish to preserve is the focus of their interest. To what degree do they permit their own personal interest (in the research of this object) to interfere with the illustration of the full richness of that object? The ideal outcome of research must be the result of combined efforts and intentions. If that does not happen — i.e., if supporters do not "take themselves personally out of the picture" and turn the exercise into a joint effort — they will end up halfway down the road towards the assessment of that object, but without the result of having saved it.

Multi-
disciplinary

Therefore, while weighing the legal aspects of the preservation of monuments, it is necessary to remember that the preservation of monuments is a multi-disciplinary effort. It is inadequate to talk only about technology or administrative processes. As the *Venice Charter* says, the preservation of monuments is defined as a method that is based on sciences, and it is clear that it involves many professions. The following are several different spheres that the preparation of preservation law involves; they are not in the order of their importance, but more in a sequential order:

Property rights

1. The historic monument is a structural work, affected by ownership rights. Today's society is very sensitive to ownership rights. The owner has the right to freely decide the fate of a building, but the State, with the help of legislation, puts certain restrictions on that right. Protection of cultural values should be not only in the interest of the public, but also in the interest of the owner of the monument; however, heritage officials alone are not the final judges in a conflict between the economic priorities of the owner and cultural priorities. The law can create conditions, but even it cannot limit those rights too strictly without financial compensation.

Land planning

2. Cultural heritage does include monuments that are not buildings, but buildings constitute the largest part of our cultural heritage. Movable property, buildings and land are located on territories that are affected by land planning. Urbanism is a science that does research into the use of land and buildings, and it also resolves conflicts between neighbours and owners of buildings. The role of urbanism as a science is to offer information to enable objective planning and developments for the growth of cities, and for the use and organization of territory. The assessment of cultural monuments must fit into the mechanisms of land planning. The first step is the creation of a good context for the preservation of individual cultural monuments (and naturally for the protection of groups of monuments and settlements).

Construction
standards, etc.

3. Historic buildings, as buildings, fall under the jurisdiction of the building laws. Building laws address the rights and responsibilities of the property owner concerning changes and additions. These changes must conform to the building law, as well as with the preservation of cultural monuments.

Proactive
stance

4. All these features have their pros and cons. The resolution between the pros and cons is the responsibility of the public

administration, which is why the public administration must find methods of resolution. It must find ways to create a positive context for the preservation of historic monuments, so that they can be handled in a suitable manner.

Economics

5. It is necessary to consider the economic background of the whole process. People operate economically, and economic laws apply just as natural laws apply. It has often been said that the economy drives politics, but economics drives its own laws. It does so in conjunction with politics, but it has its own reasons and mechanisms. That is why, in preserving monuments, professionals must understand the mechanisms of the economic world and find out which tools to use, i.e., both positive tools and restrictive tools. If those who are involved in the preservation of cultural monuments can argue the economic aspects of the cultural heritage and the national economy, the conservation community will have more eager listeners from the financial side than if it has only cultural arguments for historic preservation.

Consumerism

6. The public administration and society have a responsibility to protect the consumer. The preservation of cultural monuments is a service that is offered by expert bodies that have the duty and experience to do this; along with the right to protect the consumer, they have the responsibility to check the quality of the work done in the restoration. This interest is not only focused on the owner, but also on the general cultural welfare. Damage caused by unprofessional building firms or by non-professional restoration practices is often greater than damage caused by neglect.

Environment

7. At present, protection of the environment is considered a larger issue than protection of the cultural heritage, so the connection between the environment and cultural monuments becomes more important all the time. Interest in cultural landscapes also includes interest in the overall environment. Protection of cultural landscapes (with a view to their content) requires special methods and tools. It is not possible to apply rules that have been used on the restoration of small accessory structures, for example, to the protection of entire cultural landscapes.

Archaeology

8. Another special problem concerns archaeological sites. Their special legal problem is the lack of clarity in their ownership status; this may be because of where they are located or the artifacts that are involved. Once they are discovered, professionals can determine what can be labelled a "monument." The law says that even the unknown (that which lies covered by the ground) can still be a cultural

monument. The special problems of archaeology also require special solutions.

Education

9. If the conservation community wants to change both realities and ideas for the preservation of cultural heritage within society, it is necessary that this work be carried out by professionals who have the proper education. Education in regard to the preservation of cultural monuments is something that is still being developed. The law alone does not specify what education is necessary for professionals to carry out the law. That problem is not unique to Central European countries. The professional training for the people who are charged with the preservation of monuments should be specialized.

The public

10. Of equal importance is the education of the public in general. The question of school information — about historic preservation, the value of the cultural heritage, or the people's own cultural heritage — is the basis for the building of cultural values. All tools — economic, legal, administrative — can work only when the general public has interest in their cultural environment and in their own cultural identity.

Culmination

Democratic societies should guarantee citizens the right to a cultural identity.

Sources for
National Strategy

*Marc Denhez**

Models for
legislation

Where does a country draw its inspiration for legislation for the protection and rehabilitation of buildings?

There is often an assumption that we start with the *Venice Charter*, but the problems with this ICOMOS document are simple:

- it is not a treaty,
- it is not a declaration by the United Nations, and
- it is not a declaration by the representatives of heads of government from sovereign states.

Official
commitments

There is, however, no shortage of more official guidelines on the contents of legislation — starting at the General Assembly of United Nations.

U.N. General
Assembly

- The General Assembly has passed formal resolutions approving the *Global Strategy for Shelter to the Year 2000*, which specifically contemplates the protection of gigantic numbers of buildings.
- A General Assembly resolution also laid the groundwork of *Agenda 21*, which was the blueprint for national legislation on sustainable development approved at the Earth Summit in Rio de Janeiro in 1992. The Earth Summit was attended by the largest number of heads of state of any meeting in human history.**

UNESCO

There is also an established procedure for dealing with the *Recommendations* of UNESCO.

Treaties and
declarations

When we look at these organizations, we discover that there are indeed treaties that are specifically on the protection and

---

* Marc Denhez, a lawyer in Ottawa, Canada, is the former Research Director for Heritage Canada, chairman of the Legislation Committee for ICOMOS Canada, and chairman of Canada's committee on the future of the residential renovation industry.
** To this list, one could now add *The Habitat Agenda,* adopted by the second United Nations Conference on Human Settlements (Habitat II), Istanbul, June 1996. *Ed.*

rehabilitation of buildings and formal international declarations that, without being treaties, still have high-ranking approval by the governments of sovereign states.

Three
viewpoints

Those documents deal with buildings from three perspectives:

- housing,
- heritage, and
- sustainable development.

Subject-matter: Six
topics

When reviewing those documents, it is possible to categorize these guidelines into six major areas:

1. physical planning;
2. protection of buildings from damage caused by the State itself;
3. encouragement of the State's own re-use of buildings;
4. State controls on the damage caused by the private sector (citizens and corporations);
5. State encouragement, for the private sector to re-use buildings properly; and
6. creation of a positive climate for private citizens to work together for the re-use of buildings, without direct State intervention.

These appear to be the six areas that any national strategy should address.

Shortage of
national
"models"

If a country decides to develop a complete legislative strategy, where does it look for models? What countries have introduced a complete strategy that can be easily imitated? The answer is that nobody has.

Historical
background for
shortage

The problem is that most western countries now realize that many of their old models were a mistake. The turning point appears to have come in 1987 when an international commission headed by Gro Harlem Brundtland, the prime minister of Norway, concluded that the previous way of doing development was not sustainable. According to this well-publicized report, the world had to find a new way to do sustainable development, entirely different from what had been done for the previous fifty years. This requires explanation.

Previous
approach:
"Planned
Obsolescence"

In 1929, the Great Depression started. Many industrialized countries were devastated, and some theorists argued that to ensure there would always be enough demand for industrial production, a country should arrange (in advance) that produced goods should be constructed to fall apart and need replacement soon. This theory, called "Planned Obsolescence,"* meant that

---

* Although the expression "Planned Obsolescence" was coined in 1956, the concept was familiar decades earlier.

industrial societies should make sure that the economic life of their investments was as short as possible.

Legislative
entrenchment
of Planned
Obsolescence

At first, this was just a theory, but World War II changed that. In many countries, new tax systems had to be introduced, to finance the war effort. Once the tax systems had been introduced, accounting systems had to be adjusted to fit with the new taxes. The designers of the new tax systems (and the accountants who worked with them) were influenced by the major economic theories at that time. One of the theories that influenced them was the one just described, Planned Obsolescence, which meant that buildings (along with all other investments) were supposed to be replaced as soon as possible. That theory was supported by many of the architectural theorists and urban planners of the time.

Effects on
accountancy

It is therefore no surprise that for the next fifty years, the accounting system in many countries was slanted toward the replacement of property, instead of towards the repair of property. Anyone who was trying to calculate the profitability or the competitiveness of any investment was influenced by accounting and tax rules that said that

- buildings were expected to fall apart;
- owners would have a tax problem if they tried to sell a building before it had fallen apart;
- when a building was destroyed, the owner "lost" the building, as if it had floated away; this "loss" would affect taxable income, so taxes would go down every time a building was destroyed.
- On the other hand, the rehabilitation of buildings was not favoured, because these buildings were considered obsolete to begin with and not worth preserving. The accounting rules and tax rules surrounding rehabilitation were either unfavourable or impossible to understand.

In the meantime, a giant set of legal measures was established to favour new construction and the replacement of older buildings after the war. These rules were built into

- the accounting system,
- the planning system and
- standards of construction.

Effects on
construction
standards

For example, standards of construction were usually designed with only new buildings in mind; if an owner wanted to make an old building as safe as new construction, many countries refused permission unless the building also had the same materials and dimensions as new construction; this made the repair project impossible.

The international community was making these kinds of mistakes not only with buildings; by the 1980s, countless observers were pointing out that countries were making the same mistakes with almost every other product of industrial society. This is part of the reason the international community decided that it was time to look at how countries undertook development. This is why the United Nations General Assembly voted in 1989 for a world conference to address this problem; that is what led to the Earth Summit in Rio de Janeiro, and *Agenda 21*.

At the same time, the United Nations was also re-examining the question of housing, and the problem of "sustainability" was raised in its publication *Global Strategy for Shelter to the Year 2000*.

1989 also saw gigantic historic events in Central and Eastern Europe. Many countries changed their political and economic systems. Although no one can predict exactly what the final result will be, it is generally agreed that nothing will be the same again. But the problem is this:

- In many countries, the future of their buildings will no longer be in the hands of officials;
- it will not be in the hands of architects or urban planners;
- it will be in the hands of accountants.

This is the challenge facing countries not only in Central Europe but elsewhere.

The first question the accountants will ask about any building is this:

- Does the building compete well with other possible uses of that land?
- In other words, is there some other use for the land that will make more money?

This question confronts any country with an immediate problem. Every country on earth has many buildings that were never built to be "competitive" in the first place. These buildings include religious properties, palaces, monuments that were built for pure glory or for military or other purposes that no longer exist.

- There is no hope of protecting these structures by making them "competitive." They require the direct intervention either of the State or of some other organization that is dedicated to their protection and ongoing maintenance.

To implement this protection, legislation usually creates a governmental veto on various activities by the owners or users of the site.

Inadequacy of
that response
for government
However, in many countries, the government is responsible for more destruction of important heritage property than the private sector is. This creates a difficulty, because the government is then in what is called "a conflict of interest": one agency may be trying to protect the site, but another agency (and often a more powerful agency) is trying to do something different. This means that the

Importance of
government
procedures
legislation must clearly include a proper procedure, to guarantee that there is a proper review for any government project that threatens the property.

- Government buildings are in a slightly different category. Some people assume that government offices, courthouses and other such buildings do not need to be competitive. That assumption is not entirely reliable because many government property managers do want them to be competitive.
- The necessity for competitiveness is even more obvious in buildings belonging to the private sector.

Scope of the
issue
In a typical industrialized country, there is one building for every three inhabitants. This includes buildings of every description: governmental buildings, commercial buildings, residential buildings, industrial buildings, etc. In the case of the overwhelming majority of these buildings, they will be protected and rehabilitated if this looks like a good investment. But if those buildings look like a bad investment, they will not be rehabilitated and eventually, they will be turned over to the pigeons or to the fire department or they may be demolished. In many places, this is as true for government offices as it is for buildings owned by the private sector.

Is heritage a
"bad invest-
ment"?
If the buildings appear to be a good investment, then they will probably enjoy *de facto* protection, because their owners will want to see them protected and rehabilitated. For decades, however, many people in the heritage conservation movement made an extremely pessimistic assumption: they believed that most heritage buildings were bad investments, that heritage buildings could not compete naturally, and that they were not economical. This led them to demand legislation that would do two things:

Traditional basic
strategy
1. provide a veto on private sector activities that might threaten the property; and
2. provide grants, subsidies, tax incentives or other economic features, supposedly to "counterbalance" the "natural" disadvantaged position of these older properties.

Origins of that
legal strategy
Although this kind of legislation has been seen mostly in the twentieth century, it actually has an extremely long history. The first legislation of this kind was adopted by the Roman Empire

in A.D. 457. Eventually, this legislative strategy developed two distinct approaches.

One basic tactic:
Lists

One approach was introduced in 1666, when Sweden invented a system of inventory for its individual heritage properties. (Later, a similar approach was applied to entire districts at a time.) Countries that follow this model usually prepare detailed lists of their heritage properties, and the exact descriptions of these properties are committed to writing. These individual properties are then protected.

Alternative tactic:
Genus

A different approach was developed elsewhere. Instead of identifying individual properties on the list, a government would pass legislation that would protect an entire class of properties. In Austria, for example, all buildings in religious use are automatically protected, even if they are not on a list yet. The most dramatic example of this kind of legislation is in Turkey, where legislation protects over fifty different categories of property. For example, if a building was a caravanserai or a fort, then it is automatically protected.

Alternative legis-
lation for housing

A third kind of legislation, on a different foundation, emerged in the nineteenth century with urban planning rules. For example, these rules often deal with housing; in many countries, laws were passed for the protection of housing even when this housing had nothing to do with that country's policy towards heritage buildings.

"Environmental"
legislation

A fourth category of legislation evolved from environmental protection. This legislation was particularly well-suited to control government projects (or other major projects) that threatened nature, and gradually, this legislation was applied not only to the natural environment, but also to the built environment.

Legislation for
"sustainable
development"

A fifth kind of legislation deals with "sustainable development." This approach is still in its infancy, but it is possible to describe the basic philosophy. It is different from what countries have seen until now.

The basic problem with most of the legislation described is that it starts with one crucial assumption: that older buildings are already uncompetitive, and that the only way to save them is by

- interfering with the owner's decision, and/or
- offering artificial economic incentives to buy the owner off.

The objective of "sustainable development," on the other hand, is to develop ways for an economy to go in the direction that conservationists usually want, all by itself.

This objective would lead a government strategy to adopt the following tactics:

Alternative
approach

1. The country would examine all of its existing legal and economic policies, particularly to identify the ones that were artificially designated for planned obsolescence. There are many "artificial" policies now that had this objective.
2. The country would then eliminate the artificial policies that were connected to planned obsolescence, so that investments will have a longer economic life expectancy.
3. This should lead to more economic forces working naturally in favour of national goals, instead of working against them.
4. The country would do its best so that its investments could be protected and re-used by the people, without the State needing to intervene with a veto or with money.

This would mean that the national strategy for buildings would be the same as the national policy towards health:

- Protective legislation would be like a hospital: it would be well-designed and effective, but reserved for exceptional cases.
- The higher national priority is to make sure that people do not get sick in the first place, and that they can take care of themselves. Similarly, with buildings, the strategy is to create a legal and economic climate for buildings to be properly taken care of by their owners, without ever needing emergency intervention.

To do this, a country must remember five things:

Alternative
philosophy:
Five parts

- First, the difficulties faced by buildings are part of a larger problem of development and the human environment in industrial societies.
- Second, the difficulties faced by buildings have specific causes. Some are "natural" — but many are artificial. A country cannot develop national strategies for buildings unless it understands those specific causes and works to eliminate them.
- Third, the international community is working together to reach solutions.
- Fourth, the international community has already produced a long list of recommended tactics. These make up an extremely important first step. They go an immense distance beyond the old policies of government vetoes and subsidies.
- Finally, the new international declarations reflect international confidence that it is possible to give new direction to the way that the world undertakes development. It is possible for populations to do positive things on their own, if

- they are not blocked by out-of-date laws and economic theories, and
- countries make it as easy as possible for them to do the right thing.

Countries will never solve all the problems this way — but they can solve most and can develop special tactics to deal with the rest. There is no shortage of tools. The task ahead is research, analysis and strategy.

Participants' Questions

Q: *If the basis of the economies of many western countries has been consumption (for the last half century), what becomes the basis of the economy in a change towards sustainability?*

A: I see no magic formula. The argument expressed at the Rio Conference was that many of our problems were ultimately caused by mathematics, i.e., that the western world had developed accounting systems whereby existing investments had to be turned over as quickly as possible, and that this had been an arbitrary decision: if the accounting systems had been set up differently, we would have reached a different way of doing business. Therefore, many of the recommendations that came out of the conference in Rio de Janeiro specifically addressed how countries can rewrite their accounting systems so that they represent the economic potential of existing investments more accurately. This is easier said than done, because the accounting systems are tied to the tax system: it is impossible to rewrite one without rewriting the other. There is nobody in the world that I know of who thinks that this can be done in less than ten years. That is the bad news.

The good news is that countries that are rewriting their entire economic system right now are not starting from fifty years behind (as we sometimes hear from some pessimists in Central and Eastern Europe); they are, in fact, rewriting their economic systems at exactly the same moment that the rest of the world is rewriting its economic system, so in that sense we are all in the same boat. That is as much as can be predicted right now. No one knows how long it will take for the international community to have an accounting system and an economic system that are more fair towards the investments that society has already made. The largest tangible product that our civilization can produce is a city, and if countries cannot find ways of bringing sustainable development to buildings, neighbourhoods and cities, that means that this entire international initiative would be doomed to failure, a prospect that is unacceptable.

Q. *In some countries like the United States, whole categories of buildings have sometimes become "unfashionable" in terms of architectural history. Economics may be a crucial factor in the background, but there was a period (certainly in the 1950s, and even later in some parts of the country), when even later Victorian building was simply considered ugly and so out of fashion that to destroy it was to "perform a public benefit." Doesn't the influence of architectural fashions have to be factored in at some level?*

A. Indeed Canada is a striking example of that point. In 1943, the influential principal of McGill University gave a speech to Canada's association of architects in which he said that it was a "misfortune that none of the Canadian cities have yet been levelled by the war," but they need not worry, because "as soon as the war is over," the decision makers themselves would "wipe out much...from one end of this (country) to the other." As it turned out, "taste" and "economics" were linked, because by the time Canada had finished rewriting our tax system, it was written in such a way that a building was presumed to lose three-quarters of its value within the first ten years, and the demolition of a building was considered so good that the tax authorities gave it better tax treatment than if the same building were donated to charity. Finally, the process of rehabilitating buildings was considered so irrelevant, so insignificant for the national future, that it was not even defined in the Income Tax Act; to this day (1994) even tax officials are still not exactly sure what the tax treatment is for the restoration of a building.

One of the questions that comes up in every country is that of financial "incentives." Another question (which is on the minds of many people in Central Europe) is: "In the future, where is the money going to come from?" As soon as those questions are raised, the Pavlovian reflex is usually that there must be some kind of government fund, large enough for the country to continue doing good things with old buildings, and if it is not possible to establish a huge government fund with cash, then there must be a system of artificial tax rules, so that the owners of special historic buildings, by doing things with those buildings, will get some tax benefits that they would not get if they were the owners of any other kinds of buildings. Those two approaches are important, but they are not the only ones. First, let us look at the accounting system used in a country to calculate profit: it could become a larger tool for restoration than all the artificial measures put together. For example, if restoring a building to its previous condition (i.e., its status quo ante) is entirely deductible normally (from the calculation of profit), then the system will be providing a better tax climate for restoration than almost anything else one can think of. Similarly, if a country finds ways of eliminating all the existing barriers that stand in the way of people restoring buildings — and every country has built huge sets of these barriers over the last fifty years — then the country may be capable of creating a much more favourable climate for the re-use and the restoration of these buildings.

The beauty of such a strategy is that no one can accuse the country of doing something "artificial." The strategic problem in many countries is that when they introduce an artificial fund that is created for one purpose and that is not available to other people, whether it is for the restoration of monuments or for any other social or cultural purpose — i.e., if the country creates an artificial tax incentive that is labelled as "special" and "different" — then it means that in the next austerity budget, this label serves as an invitation to the people who want to cut government spending: the label of "incentive" is like asking the Minister of Finance to look at this program first. When a country decides that it wishes to deal with the economics of older buildings, it is tactically preferable to make the program look as "natural" as possible. The more "natural" it looks — the less it looks like an "artificial incentive" — then the less is the vulnerability to having that measure eliminated by some future minister of finance.

Q. *Many of the people working in historic preservation in Central and Eastern Europe face conditions very different from North America. We have governments that cannot even decide among themselves whom to name as minister, what committees to name, and whom to put on that committee within the parliament — or we have countries in the midst of civil or international war. In these cases, even with the best intentions and the wisest historic preservationists, we have to keep working with what we have. In the interim, can you think of some smaller incentives or action plans that can circumvent stalled government approval processes?*

A. The international declarations were indeed drafted by people who were aware of this problem; they had to be drafted not only with a view to the northern hemisphere countries, but also the southern hemisphere countries, which sometimes have worse problems than Central Europe. The entire planning mechanism in many developing countries is in a state of total paralysis. How do you develop strategies that can circumvent this problem? *Agenda 21* and the *Global Strategy for Shelter* identify many different tactics that can be developed strictly for the local level, that can be put into action locally, without the obligatory intervention of central governments.

The document called *Capitalizing on Art, Heritage and Culture* (published by the Federation of Canadian Municipalities) provides examples of what municipalities (i.e., local governments) in my country do to deal with these kinds of questions strictly on a local level. The international documents also place a tremendous amount of emphasis on developing associations of citizens who can work in parallel and be complementary to the government. These associations, composed of citizens who are working strictly because they are interested and because they are committed, can do various things that would not be feasible for the government itself.

Finally, there are other countries in the world (e.g., Canada) that are trying to use industrial associations, mainly the large groups of contractors. The invariable conclusion is that it is absolutely essential for any group (at the national, regional or local level) to develop a strategy. They have to have a clear idea, as Mr. Kilián stated, of their objectives and their priorities. They have to have a clear idea of the tools at their disposal and when to put them into motion. I agree that if the countries of Central and Eastern Europe simply wait until things somehow become magically clear, the results could be most unsatisfactory. We just have to plough ahead and somehow muddle through; the amazing thing about this is that when people are committed to doing so, they can usually succeed.

Q. *How do we quantify the profit from the cultural heritage? Taxes are unpopular for politicians, but do you think there is any possibility to show that the money invested in the cultural heritage can bring additional tax income for the state, e.g., via cultural tourism?*

A. This question raises two points. First, we must collect all of that data. Indeed, it is possible to assemble a strong case — and many countries have done this, to prove mathematically that investment in older buildings has a phenomenal effect upon a national economy. In my country, for example, $1 million work in renovation creates twice as many direct jobs as $1 million of work in new construction; it has a much better effect on municipal economies; and this is so even before we quantify the effects of cultural tourism. If preservationists do not put together that economic case, economic officials will throw them out the door. The problem, realistically, is that while preservationists are putting together their case to show how important they are for the national economy, everyone else in the country is putting together their own case (to show how they are important for the national economy), so we are competing for attention and may run into tax officials who reply, "Yeah, that's what they all say." Indeed, we pay tax officials precisely so that they can say no to all kinds of people who come through the door asking for special treatment — this is part of their job. The conservation community must be very well-prepared. If it wants the materials, it will find them. But do not expect miracles. Conservationists will have to work hard to capture the attention of tax officials and will have to work even harder to persuade them that they should give us any attention that they don't give to somebody else.

Q. *Are there legal instruments that not only protect the immediate envelope of the building, but that also extend to protect the surroundings of the building?*

A. In most laws in Europe and the Americas, the usual pattern is to ensure that there is a description of the property in the local land office. That description will typically say that the protection applies not only to the building, but to the lot (however described) that the building is located on, so the entire piece of real estate as it is described in the land office will be the protected area. If there is anything on that piece of land (a building, a fountain, a pond, etc.), then that is all part of the protected space.

In addition to that, in French law there is also a radius around the protected space that is also a protected zone of a certain number of metres. In the numerous countries that use the French law as a model, a varying number of metres away from the property is part of this protected zone.

Protective Legislation
in an International Perspective

*Lisbeth Saaby**

Importance

In view of the rapid changes in society and increasing internationalization, the preservation of the physical cultural heritage is not only a matter of national protection and management, but it also has an important international perspective. The national basis - which may differ from country to country, owing to different cultures, traditions, and political and economic developments - is being shaped more and more in the European and world communities. These offer

- a complementary protective framework and - not least -
- inspiration, initiative and guidance.

National level

At the national level, the protection and management of the cultural heritage should be established largely within the legal framework. This would mean (in the case of Denmark, for instance) implementing the Preservation of Buildings Act, the Planning Act and the Nature Protection Act.

Example

A few major elements are imperative for the protection of any category of cultural heritage. They might be deduced from an analysis of the possibilities for protecting "historic gardens," which constitute a category of cultural heritage positioned somewhere between buildings and landscapes (having recently been recognized as monuments in their own right). In a way, therefore, they pose a challenge to traditional protective instruments and are an interesting test of the criteria for identifying categories and values, and the appropriate design of a protection instrument.

For an apt and adequately designed protection instrument, it seems important that

* Lisbeth Saaby is a conservation consultant in Virum, Denmark. With her degree in law and her administrative background, she has served on many national and international commissions, including the Executive Committee of ICOMOS (Paris).

21

Approach
- the underlying interest be clarified,
- different interests not be covered by the same instrument,
- the characteristics of the object be taken into account when designing the instrument and, finally,
- the degree of intensity of control be developed on the basis of practice rather than according to legal provisions.

International support

In what way can the international system legally and financially provide complementary protection for the physical cultural heritage? Increasing internationalization includes

- more intensive information flow,
- the creation of an international atmosphere and exchange, and
- an increasingly shared feeling of responsibility for the works of art of humanity - regardless of frontiers.

An exception obviously exists for crisis areas where the cultural heritage has been destroyed during wartime. It is hard to accept that monuments, representing symbols of cultural identity for one party, are being used as targets for destruction by the other. This is a circumstance that emphasizes the need for international protection.

Key contents

The protection of the cultural heritage, offered within the framework of the international community, depends on different factors.

Nature of authority
- The scope, nature and status of the drafting organization must be mentioned — for example, this could be European (regional) or worldwide, which means that different international instruments could target the same aim but in a different manner.

Nature of instrument
- The nature of the statutory document (or reference text) must be noted, especially with regard to the binding effect on the states; e.g., is it a convention, a recommendation, a charter, a directive, a program? In strictly formal terms, only a convention ratified by a state and a regulation (or directive) from the European Union are binding on the states.

It is not possible to examine all the existing organizations or documents that provide a framework of possible protection. The most relevant ones are

- The Council of Europe,
- The European Union,
- Europa Nostra,
- UNESCO and
- ICOMOS.

European situation   European unity stems from its origins in one and the same civilization, and it can be strengthened by the re-appraisal of its heritage and further comprehension of what it represents. At the same time, the diversity of European culture has to be taken into account. The interchange of ideas and concepts, and the effort of developing conservation policies, may serve as a basis for adapting national legislation.

Council of Europe   After a long time — about twenty years at least — co-operation in the field of architectural heritage matters finally received legal international confirmation at the international level, in the adoption of the *Convention for the Protection of the Architectural Heritage of Europe* (Granada Convention) in 1985. This constitutes a new framework for co-operation for the Member States of the Council of Europe and, where appropriate, other states. (The revised *European Convention on the Protection of the Archaeological Heritage* is much more recent, dating from 1992.) The Granada Convention sets out some protective measures to be implemented in each country:

List of necessary laws

- The convention describes certain minimum requirements for legal arrangements based on the principle that cultural heritage must not be altered or demolished.
- The system provided for is prior authorization: it presupposes private ownership, but in principle is equally applicable to publicly owned buildings.
- Authorities are permitted to require the owner of a protected building to carry out work (or can itself carry out such work if the owner fails to do so).
- Authorities are allowed to make a compulsory purchase of a protected property.
- In their ratification, the states can declare that they reserve the right not to comply with these last two provisions.
- Moreover, the Convention provides for the obligation for the State to provide financial support (within the limitation of the budgets available).
- It also proposes the inclusion of certain elements in the national conservation policy, notably integrated conservation.

Expanding definitions   In all documents (whatever their nature), the cultural heritage is identified, definitions are given, and criteria set out for selection or evaluation.

- For many years, the definitions varied from organization to organization.
- However, the Granada Convention conforms to the idea that the affected institutions should adhere to other well-established definitions — in this case the definitions of the World Heritage Convention.

- In addition, the choice of definition might reflect the evolution of concepts, i.e., that European concepts for definitions (for monuments, groups of buildings and sites) are continuously expanding. At present, one of the main thrusts of the Council of Europe has been to introduce new concepts and arouse interest for categories of cultural heritage not yet regarded as part of "heritage" in the classic sense.

Exchanging
expertise

Meanwhile, one of the Council's important activities of a more practical nature is its technical assistance program for integrated conservation. It involves sending experts from European countries to help any national, regional and local authorities that so desire to resolve complex problems relating to the conservation and enhancement of their architectural heritage.

Success

The increasing number of Eastern and Central European states joining the Council of Europe — and acceding to the Convention — demonstrates that they believe (quite rightly) that their cultural heritage will be better protected in the process. This work comes under the headings of promoting the European cultural identity, and of seeking responses to major problems confronting society, two of the Council's present stated objectives.

The European
Union/ European
Community

For nearly twenty years now, that other European organization, the European Union (formerly European Community), has also been working to preserve the cultural heritage and even now is preparing intensified action within this field on the basis of Article 128 of the *Maastricht Treaty*. The main aims of this Article, in relation to the cultural heritage, are

Maastricht oblig-
ations

- to preserve the cultural heritage,
- to raise heritage awareness among citizens and professionals,
- to encourage exchanges, and
- to create an environment favourable to the preservation of heritage.

Targeted
property

The question of defining the heritage that European Union actions should target is difficult because the definition of heritage has evolved and expanded significantly in all countries over the last decades. What is "European Heritage"? For example, the question has been raised of whether the *World Heritage List* should be used or priority should be given to large works of restoration. To date, the intention is not to start over again with new definitions of the concepts, but to accept the existing approach that respects the heritage in its diversity.

National
priorities

So far, it is also clear that the Union accepts

- the predominant role of the Member States in this area, and
- the so-called "subsidiarity" of Union action.

This means that in terms of real legal protection, possible binding provisions stemming from a directive were not possible because the actions in the field (prior to the Maastricht Treaty) had no legal basis.

Co-operation

Naturally, it is stated that co-operation with other international fora (notably the Council of Europe) should be a priority. In principle, the Union might sign the Granada Convention, although it is doubtful whether it will do so. What is more likely is that those countries that are not members of the Union (especially those that are going to become members in the future, such as the Eastern and Central European states) will be invited to participate in specific activities.

Example: Movables

For example, in the context of cultural co-operation with the countries of Central and Eastern Europe, one may explore the possibility of introducing measures to prevent the illegal export of works of art from these countries to the Union, as well as a mechanism for stopping any illegal import into the Union.

Such measures were rendered topical by the introduction in 1993 of the "Single Market" (which was to comprise an area without frontiers) accompanied by a *Council Regulation on the export of cultural goods*, and a *Council Directive on the return of cultural objects* unlawfully removed from the territory of a Member State.

Two characteristic dimensions in the field of cultural heritage protection, including the Council of Europe's activities, are

- the financial support system - complementary in terms of the money available; and
- the direct contact between the Union and the citizens in the different countries.

Examples

The best-known program is the one that supports pilot projects to conserve the Union's architectural heritage. In recent years, projects from Poland, Slovakia, the Czech Republic and Hungary have been included. In order to highlight certain aspects of the conservation of cultural heritage (and to make more efficient use of Union resources), the Commission decided to concentrate on annual themes such as the 1995 theme of religious monuments. A large number of applications have been submitted each year, and by means of an evaluation process up to 100 have been selected. This kind of European subsidization is an incentive for national restoration activities and very often acts as a catalyst for national and international funding. In future, the scheme might be redesigned to give it a more international European flavour and a less top-heavy administration for the benefit of national institutions and the Union alike.

Europa Nostra

Altruistic non-governmental organizations (NGOs) also play an important role. The grass-root movements can be the exponents and creators of awareness about preservation, both among the population and *vis-à-vis* public authorities. In contrast to the Council of Europe and the European Union, Europa Nostra is a non-governmental organization (consisting of over 200 voluntary European preservation societies, local and individual members), with the aim of conserving and protecting the architectural and natural heritage. Its best-known activity is the annual award scheme, started in 1978. Recipients of the award are chosen on the basis of two criteria: architectural restoration of old buildings and adaptation of old buildings for new uses. By presenting the awards to a few houses every year from almost every country — with the eager attention of the media — it has raised preservation awareness. The Europa Nostra Restoration Fund also directs financial support to restoration projects organized every year on a specific theme.

UNESCO

Moving from the European to the global scene, the most important organizational protective framework is UNESCO's, with three conventions and ten *Recommendations*. All three conventions have played a part in protection efforts at both international and national levels. The most successful and best-known one is the *Convention Concerning thr Protection of the World Cultural and Natural Heritage* (World Heritage Convention) of 1972. As an international protective instrument, it is the world's most ratified agreement on conservation.

World Heritage Convention

The Convention enshrines the principle that the most precious treasures of humanity's cultural and natural heritage are a shared trust and are therefore our shared responsibility. The Convention specifies that Member States shall enact certain principles of planning to integrate sites of great heritage importance "into the life of the community" and will create certain laws and agencies for this common legacy.

World Heritage List

The Convention also provides for the creation of a "World Heritage List" comprising both cultural and natural heritage.

- The States in which these "listed sites" are located undertake to put in place all legislative and administrative measures necessary to ensure that such properties are properly preserved, protected and managed. At present, there are about 400 properties on the list, predominantly cultural. They span the whole globe.
- The procedure for inclusion on the list is complicated. Member States submit detailed nominations to the Secretariat of the Convention, which is provided by UNESCO. The nominations are scrutinized and evaluated on criteria carefully drafted with the assistance of the two non-governmen-

tal organizations: ICOMOS for cultural properties and the International Union for the Conservation of Nature (IUCN) for natural properties.

Criteria
- Cultural properties can qualify under six criteria relating to "outstanding universal value": unique artistic achievement; an achievement that has exerted great influence on the development of architecture; monumental arts or town planning and landscaping; testimony to a now extinct civilization; a type of building or human settlement that has become vulnerable under the impact of change; and one associated with events or beliefs of outstanding universal significance. Furthermore, all nominations must provide convincing evidence of a high degree of authenticity, a satisfactory approach to conservation and an effective management plan.

World Heritage in Danger
- In addition to the World Heritage List proper, there is also a shortlist called "World Heritage in Danger." World Heritage Sites may be threatened and may require urgent safeguards. The risk may be natural - as in the case of Kotor, shattered some years ago by an earthquake, or man-made, as with Dubrovnik.

- The international community's recognition, in the form of publicity and moral support, is imperative but may be not sufficient. The Convention therefore provides for the World Heritage Fund, which enables concrete financial and technical assistance to be offered for identifying sites, expert advice, training and emergency assistance for endangered listed sites. The intention is to create a system for raising the funds for large-scale operations (in some cases connected with the launching by UNESCO of an international campaign). So far, the Fund's financial resources have mostly been allocated to the Third World, not to Europe.

- One of the obvious benefits of international listing is to strengthen the hand of those at a national level who are committed to protection, e.g., conservation staff (who have to compete with other government agencies for limited funds), local authorities or even private associations of concerned people. It is the clearly stated expectation of the Convention that Member States that nominate sites for international recognition should also match the commitment and responsibility of the international community.

Delinquent states
- However, as examples have shown, these expectations are not always met: some states seem to forget their responsibility once they have obtained the publicity or development turns out to be more complicated and difficult than envisaged. In some cases, therefore, states have failed to fulfil their obligation to protect and conserve the monuments in good condi-

tion and in harmonious environments unaffected by pollution in a broad sense. During the Convention's Twentieth Jubilee in 1992, the question was raised of whether a revision of the Convention was appropriate to introduce provisions binding the states to their responsibilities, i.e., the states have to recognize that the global community has joint responsibility that leads to a certain control — as well (naturally) as a willingness to assist. It was decided that the change called for in the States' approach should be sought by improving the way the Convention is implemented, rather than by revising it. Thus, concern for the sites does not cease when they are admitted to the list.

Monitoring procedures have been established, both regularly and in response to new threats. These procedures have recently been improved, in collaboration with ICOMOS, and to a certain extent are based on the flow of information on conservation matters that passes through this organization and other channels.

Several subjects might deserve special monitoring even though various conditions were supposed to be met at the time of admission. These include:

- lack of legal protection (e.g., following the transfer of ownership from the State to the church or a private owner),
- lack of concern for physical deterioration of the site, unauthorized alterations, removal of objects, offensive action to the buffer zone around the site, etc., and
- bad management of tourism requirements, etc.

Reports made by experts are presented to the states and negotiations between UNESCO, the World Heritage Centre and the states are starting, in order to find solutions. In that way, the protection of World Heritage monuments will assume a more dynamic character, in accordance with the aims of the Convention.

Another treaty, the UNESCO *Convention for the Protection of Cultural Property in the Event of Armed Conflict*, was adopted at the Hague in 1954 with the best of intentions, but unfortunately has proved ineffective in more than 100 wars in different parts of the world since its adoption, most recently in parts of the former Yugoslavia. According to a comprehensive review of the Convention that UNESCO commissioned in 1993, these losses have in most cases been due to the failure of parties to comply with international law and to respect and positively safeguard the heritage.

What is needed is greater recognition, acceptance and application of the provisions in peacetime, during the preparatory work and in wartime, by all parties. The acknowledged correlation between the physical evidence of the culture of a people and its national culture and ethnic and spiritual identity has led to the deliberate destruction of that physical evidence. Understanding and respect for the cultural symbols and values of all peoples is essential in order to remedy such deplorable actions.

With regard to the Hague Convention's definition of cultural property, it is noteworthy that it covers both immovable (monuments) and movable (museum objects), whereas the World Heritage Convention deals only with the immovable heritage. The practical provisions requested in the Hague Convention consist of

- a system of blue shields placed on the monuments to identify them for protection,
- the designation of properties for special protection,
- information and education of the armed forces, the population, etc.

World Heritage Sites, in particular, seemed to be potentially eligible for special protection; but so far, the states have not been very interested in fulfilling the requirements, both in general and with regard to the World Heritage Sites.

Possible revisions

There now seems to be a consensus emerging that the Hague Convention and its implementation need to be strengthened, possibly

- by drafting new legal provisions that could take the form of either amendments to the text of the Convention or a protocol to the Convention (more probably the latter, in order not to create problems for the old and valuable part of the text);
- by doing further preparation (in peacetime);
- by strengthening the provisions on protecting and respect for cultural property, with a number of prohibitions; and/or
- by making the so-called "Special Protection System" more objective and simple while still making use of the "International Register of Cultural Property under Special Protection."

Ongoing concerns

Yet regardless of improved provisions in the Hague Convention, it is up to the states to undertake the implementation, largely in terms of national legislation and administrative procedures. Without the appropriate sanctions, it is left to the national authority to act, while no provisions are made for the international community to take action.

Furthermore, in view of recent events in the former Yugoslavia, there should be provisions on non-international armed conflicts. They will naturally be met by concern about respect for "national sovereignty," but are important nonetheless.

Hands-on emergency assistance and supplies of restoration materials are needed. The Risk Preparedness Scheme has been set up by the organizations ICOMOS (International Council on Monuments and Sites), UNESCO, ICCROM (International Centre for the Conservation and Restoration of Monuments) and ICOM (International Council of Museums). The scheme is based on the need for first aid, preparedness and advocacy, and consists of establishing a Culture-at-Risk Fund, Blue Shield Organization, Training Scheme, Information Management Scheme and Awareness Program. The scheme is in its preparatory stage but should be operational soon.

ICOMOS

The organization that has taken the initiative for this rescue scheme, and which provides professional assistance to UNESCO in questions related to World Cultural Heritage is ICOMOS, the non-governmental organization that holds consultative status to UNESCO because of its expertise in the conservation of cultural heritage. When ICOMOS was founded in 1965 (one year after the publication of the influential *Venice Charter*), the two main aims of ICOMOS were defined as being

- to promote (at the international level) the conservation, preservation, use and management of historic buildings or ensembles and sites, and
- to promote, co-ordinate and disseminate a corpus of knowledge and experience in the preservation field.

Publications
and research

The means of achieving these aims included taking a prominent place in the field of definitions and providing follow-up texts to the *Venice Charter*. The development of professional guides (such as the 1982 *Florence Charter on Historic Gardens*, the 1987 *Washington Charter on Historic Towns*, the 1990 *Lausanne Charter on Archaeological Management* and the 1993 *Guidelines on Education and Training*) has played an important role in the development of conservation theory and philosophy on a worldwide level.

Despite the fact that, formally speaking, these charters have no binding effect on states, they do appeal to a strong sense of moral responsibility among professionals and authorities and over the years have had a sizable impact on the national and international levels of preservation.

Inspiration and guidance have been provided not only by the charters but also by the scientific work of the ICOMOS international committees on specific subjects, notably within the field of methodology. In fact, the development of professional scientific work has and always should be one of the cornerstones of the organization.

Future plan

This aspect is also emphasized in the ICOMOS *Future Plan* (1993), indicating goals, objectives and strategies for taking ICOMOS towards the next century. ICOMOS should confirm its focus on scientific professionalism by strengthening its scientific activities, improving their co-ordination, developing high-quality research and exploring new ways of establishing supplementary frameworks for dealing with scientific work.

Evolving targets

Another issue dealt with in the *Future Plan* related to the identification of the cultural heritage and conservation: how these key concepts are evolving from architectural heritage through to archaeological management, and from monuments, groups of buildings and sites, as traditionally defined, through to cultural heritage in the broadest sense of the term, even including intangible heritage and living culture.

Evolving concepts are necessarily reflected in the definitions used in the reference texts, and it is a prerequisite to efficient protection that the objects are clearly identified and defined in the statutory documents.

Conclusion: The necessity of evolution and interaction

The evolving concepts of cultural heritage (and conservation) reflect the significance for the people whose cultural heritage they set out to preserve: heritage is a symbol of the cultural identity of a people. The international protective framework has developed into a supportive and even necessary complementary framework, constituted by an interaction between different international instruments and different international organizations.

These concepts are the result of the sense of common responsibility and of increasing international collaboration and peace-keeping efforts during the last five decades.

The powerlessness to avoid the destruction of the cultural heritage has been a cruel experience, but it is the responsibility of the world community to prevent and minimize the damaging effects to the greatest extent possible. In times of peace and war alike, solidarity at the international level is necessary to create the protective and preventive measures needed to conserve the cultural heritage, bearing in mind that preservation and peace are both shaped in the minds of people.

Inventorying the Cultural Landscape and Cultural Heritage: A Methodological Case Study

Hans Peter Jeschke*

Cultural and ecological values

International organizations have undertaken laudable efforts to protect cultural and natural monuments, such that cultural values are increasingly being recognized as universal: every culture represents an expression of generally accepted values. Dialogue between international, national and regional cultures can be founded upon not only the recognition of these values, but also the common basis that they offer for mutual acceptance, appreciation, and preservation of their heritage and further development of their creative powers. Cultural along with ecological factors are gaining ever more significance and are becoming a central motive in designing, planning and developing the confines of our environment. Austria contributed to the writing of the World Heritage Convention and reflects it through its broad cultural diversity.

Austrian legislative background

Inventories

Although preservation of nature in the Federal Republic of Austria is placed under the jurisdiction of each of the nine provincial governments (*Länder*), protection of cultural heritage (concerning monuments and ensembles) is under the federal legislation. In addition to "monuments" (and groups of buildings of architectural historical interest in rural sites), it is also necessary to protect modest works that have gained cultural significance over time. To supplement the protection provided primarily to individual monuments by the federal legislation, the governments of the *Länder* and of several Austrian cities and communities have developed legal, financial and planning measures to promote townscape care (*Stadt-* and *Ortsbildschutz*) and to preserve rural sites and historic town centres.

* Hans Peter Jeschke is an engineer and Chairman of the Working Group on Regional Planning, Physical Planning and Urbanism for ICOMOS Austria. He is a senior heritage official for the province of Upper Austria.

Two provinces (Salzburg and Upper Austria) have already introduced landscape inventories. Besides other activities at the federal level, a part of the Austrian cultural heritage is already being documented by a federal monument register and in two provincial registers. Upper Austria has produced the Comprehensive Cultural Heritage Register (*Umfassender Kulturgüterkataster*), while Tyrol has developed a *Kunstkataster*.

Austrian comprehensive cultural landscape research program

The Federal Ministry for Science and Research initiated a comprehensive cultural landscape research program entitled "Sustainable Development of Austrian Cultural Landscapes" with emphasis on the following aims and objectives:

- standardized cross-frontier cultural landscape classifications employing internationally accepted (co-ordinated) methods;
- establishment of a set of instruments for defining cultural landscape development models;
- elaboration of methods (modelling, expert systems) and sets of measures for model-oriented cultural landscape development;
- development of integrated monitoring systems (with ecological, economic, social, technological and political parameters) as a precondition for comprehensively controlling changes in the landscape entity under consideration; and
- establishment of a European-wide network of cultural landscape research.
- Prerequisites for these proposed changes are as follows:
- harmonizing evaluation systems for different fields, e.g., environment, regional planning, sociology and economics;
- precedence of landscape-specific development (of individual scientific projects) to achieve a maximum of development options; and
- scientific work that places emphasis on landscape and/or regional entity harmonization ecologically, socially, and economically.

This program is now being implemented and covers several methodical projects and case studies.

Harmonize definitions

It was necessary to harmonize methods to identify cultural landscapes on national, regional and local levels. The definition of the comprehensive landscape units (geo-cultural regions) according to national and international guidelines was intended to complement the description of their specific "identity" (cultural landscape types, cultural landscape elements and the cultural heritage).

Austrian cultural landscape and heritage in the international framework

Austria has signed and ratified the *Berne Convention on the Conservation of European Wildlife and Natural Habitats*. Austria is also a member of the Council of Europe and a signatory to the *Convention for the Protection of World Cultural and Natural Heritage* (World Heritage Convention).

The latter convention defines (at Article 1) three categories of cultural property:

- monuments,
- groups of buildings, and
- sites.

Cultural properties

These types of cultural property are not isolated within a landscape but rather are an integral part of it. For maintaining the historical, cultural and art-historical expression of buildings and their environment, it is therefore necessary to introduce surrounding zones as an additional category, which can be called "Buffer Zones," pursuant to the Operational Guidelines of the World Heritage Convention. These zones would be an integral part of the property under preservation and consist of either non-developed areas such as open spaces, farmland or vineyards or areas with structures belonging to the original ambience. The third category, "sites," and the additional category of surrounding zones are directly relevant for defining and mapping cultural landscapes — i.e., works of man (or combined works of nature and of man) and areas including archaeological sites that are of outstanding historical, aesthetic, ethnological and/or anthropological interest.

Contiguous zones

Natural properties and reference to resource maps

Article 2 covers natural properties. Again, three categories have been defined:

- physical and biological formations,
- geological and physiographical formations, and
- natural sites and precisely delineated natural areas of outstanding value.

As a result of mapping a selected part for resources of the natural environment ("*Naturraumpotentialkartierung*"), it was possible to describe the interaction of "man and nature" in these "geo-cultural regions" of Upper Austria.

	Inventory Category	Spatial merits, architectural and historical merits, significance	Purpose of preservation
	A Original substance: Original buildings and open spaces forming a unit on account of very marked stylistic features characteristic of a given period or region	Outstanding spatial, architectural and historical merits Outstanding importance to the build-on site	**A Preservation of the substance:** Total preservation of all buildings and open spaces. Elimination of any disturbing elements
Sites, built in area **Ensemble**	**B Original structure:** Buildings and open spaces forming a unit on account of stylistic features characteristic of a given period or region	Obvious spatial, architectural and historical merits Obvious importance to the build-on site	**B Preservation of the structure:** Preservation of the arrangements and general configuration of the buildings and open spaces. Total preservation of the buildings and open spaces. Total preservation of individual items essential to the structure as a whole
	C Special character: Due to the buildings and open spaces with different historically and regionally typical faetures forming a unit with the old and new buildings existing	Spatial, architectural and historical merits not striking Merit to the build-on site not striking	**C Preservation of the character:** Preservation of the existing balance between the old and new buildings respectively formation of such a balance. Integral preservation of individual items important to the special character of the whole unit
View of the environment **Surrounding area**	a An integral part of the site, free of buildings or whose buildings belong to the original environment b An appreciable of the site generally built on	Outstanding importance to the site ot its constituents Obvious importance to the site or its constituents	a Preservation of special characteristics: Preservation of an open space or farming land (Cultural Landscape), conservation of plant life and old buildings important to the build-on site. Elimination of any changes which impair the site. b Preservation of characteristics which are essential to relationship with site constituents
E singular items to be protected	Outstanding importance to the site or its constituents	Outstanding importance to the site or its constituents	**A** Preservation of the substance **B** Preservation of the shape

The subject-matter of the inventory is assembled according to specific categories and a predetermined range of documentation. It is catalogued and documented within the context of a regional cultural research program, according to

	"LAND" (provincial government)-community	UNION (State)	
Built-on site area to ne protected	Sites of regional importance	Ensembles meeting the requirements of the Federal Monuments Protection Act	
	Ensembles of regional importance*		* Town-planning cataloguing in "Comprehensive Maps of Cultural Heritage" belonging to the "Land Use Register of Upper Austria", used either on the instruction for regional policy and community development respectively for advisory purpose being beyoned the decision-making nature in the sense of the Spatial Planning Act of the Upper Austria.
	Sites and ensembles of local importance*		
Surrounding area to be protected	Areas of regional importance	(Narrow surrounding concerning the objects under protection)**	** Determination by the nearest surrounding of the monument and for this reason not show cartograohically
	(Areas of local importance)*		
Singular item to be protected	Object of cultural and other importance	Monuments determined according to the Federal Monumental Protection Act	
		Sites of the archaeological interest. Discovery sites. Monuments.	

the requirements of both the Upper Austrian Built-On Sites Act and the Physical Planning Act, resulting in the "Comprehensive Register of Cultural Heritage and Built-On Sites." (Jeschke and Heusser-Keller)

Rural cultural heritage

The cultural landscape-oriented mapping of rural cultural heritage on a regional level was used on the one hand as a descriptive element, and as criteria for categorizing cultural landscape units on the other hand.

The need for a scale-sensitive framework led to a method for spatial (cultural landscape-oriented) inventory of the cultural heritage on the local level according to international criteria.

Units

To establish a comprehensive cultural landscape policy, it was necessary to portray the instrumental measure for preserving, maintaining and developing these comprehensive cultural landscape units (especially in agriculture, landscape planning and spatial planning). In order to allow the integration of the goals mentioned above (i.e., the relationship of cultural landscape units) with the regions of the Austrian land planning system, they were depicted according to the international NUT - regions of the European Union (*Nomenclature des unités territoriales statistique*), the target areas according to the EU's structural fund and spatial units of the *Convention for Alpine Preservation*.

Forecasting

In this framework, the first-time introduction of a socio-geographic categorization of local government units (according to latest methods) was used to indicate regional potential in cultural heritage units. The objective is to describe "endogenous" potential, i.e., self-generating economic potential developed by the people themselves. The depiction of the relationship between farmers (current status and prognosis) and the different cultural landscape units hints at the present and future problems in cultivating that landscape. Finally, environmentally relevant pedagogical aspects (and materials and materials for converting these results into usable teaching materials and appropriate museum items) are outlined.

Mapping cultural landscape

Definitions of cultural landscapes

The methodological objectives in Upper Austria's Project on Mapping Cultural Landscapes can be described as follows. Cultural landscapes represent the "combined works of nature and of man" designated in Article 1 of the World Heritage Convention. The revised version of the Operational Guidelines defines three categories of cultural landscapes and deals with "geo-cultural regions" and their essential, distinct elements. "Cultural landscape" therefore embraces the manifestation of diverse interaction between humankind and its natural environment.

Contents

For Upper Austria, nineteen comprehensive cultural units were methodically developed according to nationally executable criteria on the geo-cultural model. These units are assigned primarily to:

- the Bohemian massif — the granite and gneissic highlands (unit numbers A1-A6);
- the Alpine forelands (unit numbers B7-B13); and
- the northern Alpine area (unit numbers C14-C19).

Description of these units proceeded according to the following criteria:

- ecological landscape classification (cultural landscape types) together with botanic and zoological aspects;
- structural elements close to nature (cultural landscape elements such as biotops, rural orchards, etc.);
- the interaction of "man and landscape," based on the "Upper Austrian study for mapping the resources of the natural environment" (i.e., landscape-dependent recreation potential, fertility potential of soil and forestry, water system potential and raw materials potential);
- the agricultural future, including aspects and objectives of agrarian and landscape planning;
- spatial planning (NUT regions), including the *Convention for Alpine Preservation*, to reinforce and promote a comprehensive cultural landscape policy by these planning and preservation instruments;
- rural settlements and vernacular architecture;
- a socio-economic regional classification of local government units; and
- the depiction of population development (including indications of sustainable development potential in the different cultural landscape units).

Documents   Inventorying the cultural heritage was complemented by rural and urban studies based on the landscape-oriented mapping and evaluation method. The systematic compiling and dissemination of a basis for information available is complemented by the information system *Comprehensive Cultural Heritage Register and Built-On Sites (Umfassendel Kulturguterkataster)* and the *Upper Austrian Map of the Resources of the Natural Environment* together with the *Upper Austrian Landscape Inventory.*

Goals in planning   In their relationship with regional planning, landscape planning, and other instruments for maintaining and preserving cultural landscapes, three important aspects of cultural landscapes need to be assessed in the context of developing planning policies:

Principles

a) Sites are present within landscapes: sites do not exist in isolation, and site-oriented planning policies require revision so as to include elements of landscape sensitivity.
b) The cultural landscape exists in both urban and rural areas: while different planning problems exist in urban and rural

LANDSCAPE	SETTLEMENT	STREET AND SQUARE	OPEN SPACE & VEGETATION	STRUCTURES
		– flowing boundaries between the various public, semi-public, and private areas of different usage near the road	– secondary vegetation in the area surrounding the farmhouse	**"Dreiseithof"** trilateral farmhouse or gatewall-farm – U-formed farmyard, 3 sides of the yard surrounded by buildings, the fourth side closed by a wall with a gateway (as the entrance to the yard, often with an additiomal gateway for pedestrians, the so-called Gehtürl), gables facing the road

LANDSCAPE	SETTLEMENT	STREET AND SQUARE	OPEN SPACE & VEGETATION	STRUCTURES
Linear lay-out of villages – in the base and on the sloping sides of a valley, as well as in higher regions of a valley	**Linear lay-out of villages*** **"Reihendorf"** – Linear village with farmsteads in a straight row with "Waldhufenflur" – wide spaces (60 meters and more) between the farmsteads – strung-out expansion – gables facing on the village road **"Zeilendorf"** – linear village built along a road with "Hofackerfluren" – spaces between the farmsteads – gables facing on the village road	**Linear lay-out of villages*** – structure dominated by buildings – smooth site-lines (Linienführung) following the contour of the terrain – clear alignment lines	**Linear lay-out of villages** – wide expansion of open spaces – the tree as a secondary element of village shape	– low cubature of the whole farmstead (along both of the neighbouring long sides, dwellings and the stable, dowerhouse, bos grain silo, transvers barn enclosing the economic area) – cropped saddle roof of an approximately common height (angle of inclinatio 37-40%) –horizontal structuring – little plastic decoration on the frontage – details : upright windowforms, usually placed symetrically along the frontage of the building, overhanging roof – normal masonry or rendering (raf texture plaster) – separate structures (private chapels or shrines, etc.) ** without numerically less usual forms of hamlets*
Hamlet – in the base and the sloping sides of a valley, as well as in higher regions of a valley **Single farmstead** – in the base and the sloping sides of a valley, frequently also in higher regions of a valley – buildings surrounded by secondary vegetation	**Hamlet** **"Planmäßiger Weiler"** (planned hamlet) – 5 to 12 farmsteads – gables facing on the village road **Single farmstead** – building at the end of a farm driveway or as an access road – commanding site resulting from locational factors in the midst of blocks fields	**Hamlet** – structure dominated by buildings – smooth site-lines following the contour of the terrain – clear alignment lines **Single farmstead** – individual item	**Hamlet** – the tree as a secondary element of village shape **Single farmstead** – the tree as a secondary element of village architecture	

areas, it is essential to recognize the importance of the cultural landscape in both.

c) A scale-sensitive framework is needed: planning policies need to be sufficiently flexible so as to allow interpretation of the cultural landscape over a range of scales.

Example of the description, in the inventory, of rural settlements and vernacular architecture in relation to cultural landscape units A1 and A3 in Upper Austria. In this case, planners were working on principles for a regional cultural landscape unit policy model, pertaining to distribution of *Dreiseithof* (three-sided complexes) or *Tormauerhof* (gatewall farm complexes). (Jeschke and Spielhofer)

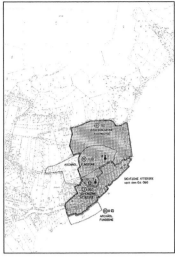

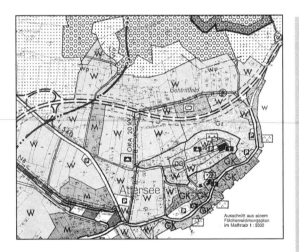

Attersee is a community in a rural area that has been inventoried. The centre of Attersee is a protected district, and along with the surrounding zone of Kirchberg, these two areas are treated as a comprehensive surrounding zone, or *Sichtzone*, according to the Built-On Sites Act of Upper Austria. These two areas are considered to have different significance: the surrounding zones are considered to be of *regional* importance (particularly for protected views, such as the view from the south, bottom) while the village centre is considered to be of *local* significance and was recommended as such to the local authorities for preservation. The land-use plan is intended to reach a balance, for example, through the dedication of grassland. (Hans Peter Jenschke)

Participants' Questions

Q. *What is the status of the results of inventorying like this? You produce a lot of data, but who uses this data and for which decisions?*

A. This project produces several layers for other measurements especially for land planning, notably special planning regions, including the EU structural funds and regional activities. In Austria, this approach to landscape cultural units is not used in regional planning, because those planners use economic regions and not natural or cultural regions as such. We have to introduce the criteria (to identify cultural landscape and cultural heritage) in a form that our colleagues of the special planning agency can understand, so that they can use the information at regional or local levels.

Q. *How much land in Austria is protected as cultural landscape?*

A. I was dealing with the "common" landscape, which we call cultural landscape. I was not speaking about special protected areas under the Nature Protection Act. Special protected natural areas still need some development in Austria. The main objective for my agency is to identify the normal cultural landscape.

Q. *Given the detailed characteristics of landscapes, in what manner do you influence the politics of urban development, and what is the mechanism that you use?*

A. In my region, there are very active communities, and some of these communities are eager to maintain their cultural heritage and cultural landscape. We can provide information for their tasks, e.g., to set up land-use programs and development programs.

Q. *In the process of inventorying, you probably found places that were interesting from a cultural point of view — for example, battlefields or burial grounds — but that were not in national parks. Does the land on which they stand belong to the government, or is the land in private hands? In Ukraine, there are places, such as battlefields, that should be preserved as historic landscapes, but who owns the landscape?*

A. In Austria, almost all of the land is private property. And we are only dealing with private investors or private persons who want to use the farmsteads and houses. In Austria, the State's task is only to define the framework, i.e., what is forbidden, not what to do. This perhaps is the main difference between old systems and more current democratic thinking. Secondly, we use some approaches just for information. We have several decision-making levels, which help to deepen public information and to give guidelines to the different investors or planning authorities and so forth.

Q. *When the maps are done, what is the formal relationship between those maps and the regional planning that is done by the planners? To what extent are the latter under an obligation to take account of the work that you have done?*

A. The Planning Act has special rules with respect to cultural landscapes or the cultural heritage. Our special planning act forces the owners and the planning authority to abide by this information.

Enns is Austria's oldest city and shows how the inventory applies in an urban area. The protected area was subcategorized to distinguish four locations (Untere Kaserne, Unteroffizierschule, Saint Lawrence Basilica and the Enns river bank). The protected archaeological area is listed as such on the map. There is a further map of individually significant cultural objects. (Hans Peter Jenschke)

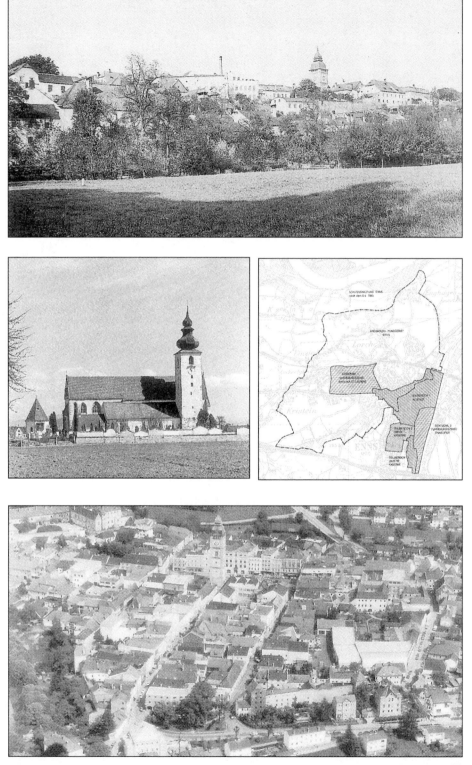

PART II:

Codes and Controls in the Public Sector

Objectives in Regulating the Structural Restoration of Historic Buildings

*Giorgio Croci**

The need for a scientific approach

The drafting and application of construction codes (and related standards) to historic buildings is challenging. Since any study of historical buildings (or planning of structural restoration) uses both

- objective data (based on mathematical models, reliable tests and surveys, etc.) and
- subjective data (direct observation of material decay and crack patterns, historical research and ancient documents, etc.),

The challenge this makes it very difficult to establish precise rules and codes. The lack of clear guidelines can easily lead to ambiguities. On one hand, it leaves room for arbitrary decisions while on the other hand, codes (which are rarely prepared explicitly for historic buildings) are often inappropriately applied.

Examples This is the case, for example, with seismic and geotechnical codes, whose enforcement leads to drastic measures, that do not respect historical values and are, moreover, not always indispensable. For example,

Incongruity
- In the ancient walls of Urbino or the clift of the Campidoglio in Rome, where parts of the original structures show large cracks and deformations, full compliance with geotechnical requirements would be incompatible with the archaeological value of the sites concerned.
- In Dubrovnik, where many historic buildings have been seriously damaged by the war, application of the Croatian seismic code would require that buildings in the area be substantially strengthened, chiefly through the use of reinforced

* Prof.Ing. Giorgio Croci is professor of Structural Restoration and chair of Consolidation of Structure for the Faculty of Engineering of the University of Rome ("La Sapienza"). He is a consulting expert for the government of Italy and on various international missions around the world.

concrete, which would involve more substantial alterations even than those produced by the shells.

Fundamentals

Although a specific code for historic buildings appears difficult to propose, some recommendations are nonetheless not only desirable, but also indispensable in order to limit the scope for arbitrary decisions and place all the relevant procedures in a rational scientific setting.

These objectives may be divided into three main types:

1. damage evaluation,
2. safety evaluation and
3. quality control.

1. Damage evaluation

The first category, damage evaluation, is based on the following main procedures:

- direct observation of a structure, with particular attention to the state of decay of materials, wear and tear, cracking patterns, etc.
- *in situ* and laboratory tests to evaluate the principal characteristics of a structure from qualitative and quantitative points of view; non-destructive tests are preferable when possible;
- monitoring systems to evaluate the evolution of some phenomena such as the width of cracks, leaning, temperature of materials, etc.;
- preparation of an overall plan of observations rather than unco-ordinated individual tests. This adds to the value of the information obtained.

Each test should also be justified on grounds of usefulness and reliability of the data acquired.

2. Safety evaluation

The second category of recommendations involves the evaluation of safety before and after intervention. Safety is not easy to evaluate; unlike designing a new building (where the objective is to prevent phenomena such as deformations, cracks, soil settlements, etc.), in the case of old buildings these may already be present.

On the other hand, the existence of the building itself allows us to have further information, from the observation of the real situation and from the historical survey.

Professionals and code officials must be ready to face certain challenges.

Procedural precautions

- A mathematical approach — which represents the main procedure in structural engineering — is not always reliable, given the uncertainties inherent in the evolution of various

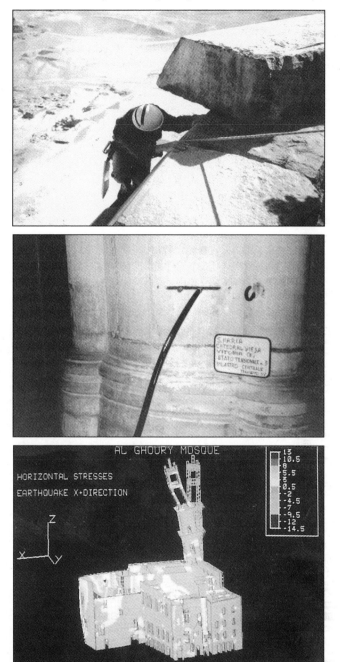

Direct evaluation should be done to assess actual damage. For example, the climber (top) is examining decay of the casing of Chephren's Pyramid at Giza; below, a flat jack test is assessing both present stresses and material strength in columns at Vieja Vitoria Cathedral in Spain. This data can be the basis for an evaluation of safety before and after intervention (bottom), but even the elastic mathematical model displayed may not give the full picture, unless it is supplemented with historical information. (Giorgio Croci)

phenomena over time, i.e., the complexity of actual structural behaviour, the difficulty of quantifying the phenomena, the effects of cracks and deformations, etc.

- Elastic mathematical models thus cannot usually explain either the cause of damages or present safety levels.
- Non-linear mathematical models, on the other hand, which can take into account phenomena that were not envisaged in the original design, are often difficult to manage and the data may not be known with certainty. It should be also borne in mind that the "objectivity" of the mathematical analysis is more apparent than real, since the structural scheme (on which the calculations are based) is often established "subjectively" and is only a rough approximation of the real situation.

Structural analysis must be supplemented

The results of a structural analysis (which is very useful for a general view of stress distribution anyway, especially in original undamaged situations) must be therefore used cautiously (in relation with the reliability of the data, hypotheses and schemes assumed). Two other criteria must integrate the information provided by the mathematical models. These two additional methods are:

- historical research, which is based on the analysis of original documents relating to past phenomena such as earthquakes, soil settlements, etc., and their effects on a monument, and

A combination of three approaches — mathematical models, historical surveys and direct observation — is the basis for the structural scheme on today's most important conservation projects, such as the Angkor complex in Cambodia. (Giorgio Croci)

- direct observation of a monument, which can determine the structural features, crack patterns, decay of materials, etc.; on the basis of observational experience over time, the weakest situations can be identified and a qualitative risk evaluation prepared.

Integration of findings

A synthesis of all the data obtainable from a critical analysis of these three criteria (mathematical models, historical survey, direct observation) is the best way to assess safety levels and to indicate the procedures for intervention.

Further risk assessment

A rational approach and defensible decisions can be assured only by a report that clearly explains

- the methodology followed, including any uncertainties and approximations, as well as
- the reliability of the data and assumptions underlying the structural analysis.

Mathematical models must therefore be considered as a more or less reliable basis for the final verdict on the safety of a building. This judgement must also indicate

- possible risk situations and
- the time limit for completion of the proposed measures.

3. Quality control

The third category, namely general criteria and quality assurance, is equally important. Although each monument has its own individual history, making it difficult to establish general criteria, it is possible to identify some general principles, which can be summarized as follows:

Avoiding overkill

- Each intervention must be decided only where a situation of inadequate safety levels has been fully ascertained, in order to avoid unnecessary interventions.
- Each intervention must respect the original concept and techniques (as far as possible).
- The "minimum intervention" approach must nonetheless take safety requirements into account.

Avoiding surprises

- Each intervention must be proportionate to the required improvement in safety levels in order to limit it to measures that are really indispensable.
- Any material used in restoration must be well known not only from the point of view of its properties, but also — and more especially — through the point of view of its compatibility with the materials used in the original building, in order to avoid detrimental side effects.

Restoration is a very delicate operation. Even where thorough investigations have been carried out, some problems will emerge and some solutions can be found only during the actual

Where work is undertaken without proper understanding of safety levels, the result can be unnecessary interventions such as the exaggerated props in the Coptic Museum after the Cairo earthquake of October 1992 (above), or unjustified alterations to the original concept such as the use of reinforced concrete in this terrace at Angkor (lower left). The use of modern materials, without an understanding of effects on earlier construction, can also produce problems such as the effects of corrosion of steel stirrups on this column at the Tabularium Palace in Rome (lower right). (Giorgio Croci)

work; this often means that it is not possible to prepare as detailed a project as in the design of new buildings, but rather only to establish general criteria as the basis for possible options to be selected, in accordance with the data acquired.

Work
staggered
or tied to
observation

When structural behaviour is influenced by evolutionary phenomena whose outcome is difficult to foresee (e.g., as can be the case with soil subsidence), restoration can be realized in successive stages, with subsequent decisions (to extend or intensify the work) being taken on the basis of the behaviour observed after the initial stages of intervention.

This approach (observational criteria) makes it possible to minimize and optimize measures in all cases where it is impossible to know *a priori* the likely effect on the phenomena of the measures being implemented.

Controls

Any intervention proposal must be linked to a plan of controls to ensure the quality of the result; measures that cannot be checked should not be undertaken. A typical example is the injection of mortars into masonry, which should be carried out only where the effectiveness of the operation can be checked by comparing the improved strength and homogeneity with the situation prior to intervention.

The leaning minaret and mosque in Samarkand will be handled by a "step-by-step intervention" to strengthen the foundation to allow maximum observation. (Giorgio Croci)

Participants' Questions

Q. *Are the craftsmen that you use in this work trained in special schools or are they trained only on the reconstruction site?*

A. There were two kinds of workers on my projects: some had no experience, while others were specialists from a local company.

Q. *Are there legal limitations on the instrumentation for diagnoses?*

A. When we are in charge of a study for a monument, we simultaneously have authorization for the investigations that are needed. We are not allowed to do investigations that could damage the monument. For example, sonic tests are not destructive and endoscopic tests are usually allowed (only 2 cm of optic fibre is inserted so usually it does not create problems). Flat jacks are different, because some cuts in the stone are required so, in short, the answer is it depends on the situation. The questions that must be asked are: (a) is it really necessary to have that data? and (b) do the characteristics of the surface allow this little alteration? There is no general rule; it depends on each case.

Q. *You described very sophisticated techniques for restoration. Many contractors/builders promise clients that theirs is the best technology for the building — for example, concrete injection — even though this may not be true. How do you respond?*

A. Italy is currently trying to prepare a formula whereby the contractors would be paid not on the quantity of the material that is inserted by injection, but for the results. If the client wants the resistance increased by 10 kg, then the contractor would be paid for 10 kg; towards that objective, the contractor would give an estimate for the improvement, and then the client monitors the result. In the meantime, the contractor can do what he/she likes. Of course, the client will check the compatibility of the materials, to avoid materials that are not compatible (i.e., with unfavourable side effects). This is a new approach. We can no longer afford the daily use of technology for which we do not know the results.

ADDENDUM (Marc Denhez)

Currently an international movement exists to change the way that codes are written. The old way that codes were written is called the "prescriptive method": that meant that if a country was worried about a risk of earthquake in a particular region, for example, it would write into its code (a) what had to be built of steel, concrete, masonry, etc.; (b) the dimensions that buildings and walls would need to have in order to meet the legal requirement. For example, the code might say that a stairwell must be made of brick and be at least two metres wide. That entire way of writing legislation is now being abandoned. The long-term intent is to replace it with what is called the "performance method": instead of saying what the materials and dimensions are, countries write into their legislation that, for example, the stairwell's materials must have a combustion point of a certain number of degrees, have a certain tensile strength, etc. We don't care what materials are used, as long as they meet that standard. It then becomes an immense task for engineers to identify all the different ways they can make the stairwell reach that level of performance. In the shorter term, some countries like Canada are working in the meantime on a third format, namely, "objective-based codes." These documents would be less detailed than "performance-based codes" about the physical characteristics that the building would need to attain; instead, the code's wording focuses on what objective is being sought for the occupant's safety, e.g., the stairwell must be capable of allowing occupants to escape within a certain number of seconds. The common intention is to ensure that the codes are written in such a way that when an existing building is repaired, the project will deliver a building that is as safe as a building built under new technology, albeit with 100 percent flexibility to use any ancient building techniques or any other building techniques that you can think of in order to achieve that safety result. There are several countries working on exactly this objective in their codes.

Impact Assessments as a Tool for Protection against the State

*Thompson Mayes**

Constant
thread

Sometimes it may appear that supporters of historic conservation encounter diverse and arcane specialties when they grapple with historic preservation problems. No one solution, no single legal approach may be appropriate in all cases, and a country may need to develop expertise as the need arises. The conservation community needs to look for approaches wherever they may be appropriate and to develop its own domestic solutions if there are no models available.

Case Study:
U.S.A.

The following is a case study of the United States' National Historic Preservation Act of 1966, which is the basic national historic preservation law in the United States. It exists in the context of complex governmental layering in the United States: there are three levels of government because of the U.S. constitution, which created a federal system of national government and state government. When the constitution was adopted, it was (for legal purposes) a grant of authority from the people to the federal (national) government:

- Only those powers that were specifically given to the national government (by the people in the document) are powers of the national government: all other powers are reserved to the states or to the people.
- The states (at the time when the constitution was adopted) were independent sovereign nations that had chosen to join together to form a federal union. The legal sovereignty of the states still exists today.
- The local system is created by a grant of power from the states to the local governments.

* Thompson M. Mayes is a lawyer and Associate General Counsel, National Trust for Historic Preservation, Washington, U.S.A.

In short, there are various sources of power, and that explains why our federal system has a layering effect. Historic preservation laws exist at all three levels and provide different protections at those levels.

The National Historic Preservation Act is a very narrow part of the strategy for dealing with historic preservation in the United States; it is only one of the components in the list of various protective measures that should be a part of any program of historic preservation. This Act is the part that deals with controlling national government action. The big surprise is that the national

government has no ability to regulate what happens on private property through the National Historic Preservation Act. When a property is listed on the National Register (described below) and there is something that private owners want to do, the National Historic Preservation Act does not prohibit them from doing anything (although local historic preservation ordinances may).

The National Historic Preservation Act created a national inventory of historic properties, called the National Register for Historic Places. The Act establishes a procedure:

- It ensures that the U. S. government "considers" the effect of its activities on historic places that are listed in or eligible for listing in the National Register.
- The protection is purely a procedural protection, even against strictly governmental actions; the Act does not require a federal agency to make a final decision that actually protects any property listed in the National Register. It requires the federal agency only to go through a procedure that demonstrates that it has "considered" the effect that its action will have on a property listed in the National Register.

This policy, which is obviously restricted, evolved from the prior laws. An understanding of these prior laws, and the context in which they were enacted, helps explain the rationale for the National Historic Preservation Act. As countries go through changes, it is essential to recognize that future policies may be improved or changed, based on the need at the time.

Prior to the National Historic Preservation Act, there were two basic federal preservation statutes. The first was the Antiquities Act of 1906, passed primarily to protect archaeological Native American sites located on lands owned by the federal government. It had no effect on private property whatsoever. It was passed largely to prevent "pot-hunters" (i.e., unauthorized people interested in artifacts and archaeological sites) from digging up artifacts from federal land and selling them. It included two key provisions:

- It authorized the federal government to designate national monuments. This Act's use of the term "monument" may be more comparable to the Europeans' use of the term than to other usage in the United States. Under the Act, the monuments were designated only on land owned by the federal government.
- The Act established a federal permit system for the excavation of archaeological sites on federal land. This was considered a radical idea in 1906.

Court tests

Eventually, the enforceability of this permit system was called into question in court cases, and conflicting decisions left doubts. Therefore, a new statute was passed in 1979 to re-establish the permit system.

"Trial and error"

It is important to recognize that if a country does not "get legislation right" the first time, it can always wait for a good opportunity to fix it.

Historic Sites Act (1935)

The second important statute that preceded the National Historic Preservation Act was the Historic Sites Act of 1935. It was passed in a dramatically different political atmosphere — the middle of the Great Depression. It focused on the recognition of nationally significant sites that would further a patriotic purpose, to build a national spirit in the United States (which was also going through an emotional depression). It was the first statute that recognized a national policy in the United States to encourage historic preservation: "[I]t is the national policy to preserve for public use, historic sites, buildings, and objects of national significance for the inspiration and benefit for the people of the United States." The policy was limited to nationally significant sites and again emphasized the patriotic purpose. Several important programs were also created, for example:

- The Historic American Buildings Survey (HABS), a program to document historic buildings that were being lost (primarily because of the economic dislocations that the country was going through). Historically, the real reason this program was created was to give work to architects and engineers who were unemployed because of the Great Depression. The program has, however, created an extremely important body of work that documents many buildings in America that have since been demolished.
- The National Historic Landmarks Program. This predecessor to the National Register for Historic Places was limited to nationally significant sites — not sites with local importance or state importance. The Act gave authority to the federal government to "exercise eminent domain" (i.e., expropriate, namely to take the property and pay compensation) on prop-

erty for historic purposes. (Prior to 1935, there was some question as to whether the executive branch of the U.S. government had the authority to expropriate property for historic purposes, without a legislative enactment in order to protect a historic site. For the first time, such authority was clearly given to the executive branch.)

Context
of 1966 Act

The historical context to the National Historic Preservation Act is again dramatically different from the historical context for the Historic Sites Act of 1935. It was passed in 1966; the U.S. government had, in the preceding decade, embarked on a massive program of public investment in the national infrastructure. Two particular programs were having a catastrophic effect on historic buildings and districts:

National
housing policy

- Urban renewal was a program that resulted from the notion that American cities were basically big slums and that the best way to eradicate the slums was to demolish the buildings, rather than to rehabilitate them. This was tied to an aesthetic value judgement that these districts, which were primarily Victorian housing, had no value aesthetically: planners would select huge areas that would be designated for demolition in order to be rebuilt anew with federal monetary assistance. Although the project may have been carried out by the city or the state, it was funded with federal money.

National
highway
policy

- American federally funded interstate highways were often built directly through U.S. cities, often resulting in the loss of gigantic blocks of historic buildings.

Rationale
Balance

In response to these federal programs, no one argued that the goals of the policies were themselves wrong — no one could argue that slums were good, and (in that era) no one argued that highway projects were bad. The National Historic Preservation Act was therefore developed as a response to try to balance federal policies. The idea behind the Act was that policies that supported the construction of new transportation projects or new housing developments could be balanced with a policy that enunciated a concern for historic preservation and historic buildings.

Shift of focus

A key part of the lobbying strategy to get the National Historic Preservation Act passed was a text issued by the Conference of Mayors and called *With Heritage So Rich*. It created an appeal on an emotional and philosophical level supporting historic preservation, a fairly new idea to most Americans at that time. The National Historic Preservation Act, which grew out of a very different historical context, had a crucially different policy from the Historic Sites Act:

De-emphasizing
"national"
significance

- it did not treat historic sites as isolated landmarks;
- the policy focused on integrating historic buildings and sites into the day-to-day fabric of American life and modern society.

Shift in scope

For example, rather than focusing only on nationally significant historic sites, the new Act broadened the sites that were protected to include those of state and/or local significance. This change represented a dramatic shift; rather than protecting nationally significant monuments only, the United States began to encourage the preservation and use of historic sites we live with everyday, and began trying to incorporate them into federal policies.

Inventory

How would this policy be implemented?

- In order to allow federal agencies to perceive their duties towards historic properties, they had to know where the properties were and what they were, so the Act created an inventory of historic properties called the National Register of Historic Places.

Agency

- The Act created a federal agency, called the Advisory Council on Historic Preservation, assigned to consult with other federal agencies and to encourage the inclusion of historic preservation in the planning of federal projects.

Process

Keystone:
"Consultation"

- A consultative procedure was created, referred to as "the Section 106 process." In the Section 106 process, federal agencies are required to consult with the Advisory Council whenever their activities would have an adverse effect on a property listed in the National Register. That is the simplest statement of what the National Historic Preservation Act actually does; it requires a consultative procedure between federal agencies about historic sites.

Breadth

Long-term
project

Currently, there are about 75,000 listings in the National Register including 6,500 historic districts, many of which include a great number of individual properties. The sites include buildings, districts, structures, objects, roads, archaeological sites, battlefields, bridges, ships, lighthouses and Native American sacred sites. The National Register is currently considered to be only about 20 percent complete.

Objective
criteria

Properties are designated through an analysis of their historic significance. Objective criteria of significance are included in federal regulations. The National Park Service, which maintains the National Register, is required to comply with the criteria in designating sites to the National Register.

Participation
of
states

The designation process typically involves the state government as well. One of the ideas behind the Act was to create a partnership between the federal government and state governments and to involve them in the federal decision-making process. Therefore the initial nomination to the National Register is begun at the state level, then is forwarded to the federal government, which makes the final decision as to whether a property will be listed in the National Register. States get some money from the federal government for doing this, but not as much as the program costs them. The states are also an essential part of the administrative process by which the consultative procedure is done. It is the state that makes an initial decision as to whether the federal agency action that is being proposed is going to have an effect on the property listed in the National Register.

Owner veto

The regulations for nomination to the National Register contain an owner consent provision. If an owner (a private owner or a public institution) of a historic site does not want it listed on the National Register, the owner may object to the listing and the property will not be listed. However, the protection included in the National Historic Preservation Act is primarily protection against other federal government actions.

Identical results

It is crucial to note that any property that is *objectively eligible* for listing in the National Register is given the same status, in terms of procedural protection from federal action, as a property that is actually *listed* in the National Register.

Scope of process

Listing in the National Register has no effect on the private property rights of a private owner: listing does not prohibit entirely private action. Concerning federal government action, however, the Section 106 process establishes a consultative procedure to ensure that federal agencies take into account the effect of their undertakings on properties listed in (or properties eligible for) the National Register, as follows:

Who is affected

- Only agencies of the national government are affected; the Act requires that those federal agencies consult with the Advisory Council.

What triggers procedure

- This procedure is triggered by an "undertaking." An undertaking includes use of property that is owned or controlled by the federal government; building a new building; altering an old building (such as when we build a new courthouse or expand a courthouse); disposition of the property at the closing of an Army base; sale or transfer of a property, such as when a bank fails and the federal government takes over property owned by the bank and then attempts to dispose of it, etc.

Federal ownership/ control

- An "undertaking" also includes entire programs that are funded by the federal government, such as when the federal government provides funds for low-income housing, for flood protection, or for the construction of a highway.

Federal
support

Federal
licensing

Federal
approval

Federal
delegations

"Effects" to
consider

Resulting
process

Contractual
protection

- An "undertaking" also includes a federal agency licensing a particular activity by either a corporation or a private individual, such as when the federal government allows wetlands to be filled in, or when it grants a licence to allow construction of a communications tower to be built, or a natural gas pipeline. In granting those licences, the federal agency is required to consider the effect the granting of that licence has on historic properties.
- An "undertaking" would also include any situation where a federal agency simply has the opportunity to approve or disapprove a project.
- Even if a federal agency has delegated to another entity its ability to approve or license some activity, that delegation (and the licence granted by the entity to which the delegation was made) is also considered an "undertaking" and therefore would trigger this consultation process.

The effects of an undertaking that are considered are very broad. An "effect" is technically defined as any change in the characteristics that would qualify a property for listing on the National Register. Any effect that changes any of the characteristics that give a property historic significance would therefore be considered an effect that could trigger the consultation process.

The federal agency that is proposing (or funding) an undertaking therefore must go through several steps.

- It must first enquire whether there is a historic property listed in (or eligible for) the National Register that would be affected.
- It then must notify the State Historic Preservation Office, which participates in the designation process and in this administrative procedural process.
- The State and the agency go through the process of determining whether the effect on the property is an adverse effect.
- If it is determined that there is an adverse effect, they go through a consultative process to try to identify ways to mitigate the effect on the historic property.
- If they reach an agreement as to how the effect can be mitigated, the federal agency will execute a memorandum of agreement ("MOA") that documents the agreement they have reached about how to mitigate the adverse effect.

In this manner and in this manner only, the National Historic Preservation Act becomes a substantive protection, i.e., through the MOA process; once the agency signs an agreement saying that the property will be treated in a certain fashion, then it is bound by that agreement. The agreement incorporates, into what is otherwise only a procedural protection, a substantive protection for the historic property.

Where no
agreement

What happens if the agency and the Advisory Council cannot agree about how to mitigate the effect on the historic property? In such a case,

- the Advisory Council on Historic Preservation is given an opportunity to comment on the undertaking. If it wishes to do so, the Advisory Council will write a letter to the head of the federal agency that is performing the undertaking and will express its concerns about the effect on the historic property.
- The federal agency does not have to accept and execute the comments of the Advisory Council as stated in the letter. The agency can simply proceed with the undertaking, which can adversely effect the historic property. The federal agency is bound only to go through this process of considering the effect that its undertaking has on historic properties; it is not actually required, unless it signs a memorandum of agreement, to do anything to protect the historic property (i.e., it can then proceed with its road construction project or its flood control project and adversely effect or destroy the property).

Political
impact

Why would the federal agency performing the undertaking not just go through the process, and do whatever it wants anyway? The answer is that it is time-consuming for a federal agency to go through this procedure. Although it is only a procedural protection, the threat of going through the procedure is often enough to make a federal agency want to negotiate an agreement to protect historic properties that are threatened. The reason the agencies do that is because they want to move their project forward quickly, whereas the procedural protection slows down the project.

Solutions

One of the advantages of the Section 106 process is that it is a flexible approach; once the negotiation process begins, the State Historic Preservation Office, the Advisory Council and the federal agency have a great deal of flexibility in determining how to mitigate the effect on the historic property. They can invent any strategy to balance the agency's goals with the Council's concern for the historic property.

Disadvantage

One of the great disadvantages of the Section 106 process is that it does not include many opportunities for public participation, which in the United States is often the most effective method of getting a federal agency or state agency to change its position about a project.

Ongoing
change

The National Historic Preservation Act was recently amended (in 1992), to cure problems that the preservation community and federal agencies had experienced in working with the Act. It is extremely important to recognize that as any government begins to enact legislation, it is quite likely to identify the need for changes in the legislation just enacted.

Conclusion

The conservation community should be prepared to go back to the various legislatures and improve the legislation that was enacted based on experiences in working with the legislation.

Participants' Questions

Q. *"NGOs" (non-governmental organizations) are increasingly emerging in Central and Eastern Europe. What are the funding sources for the National Trust for Historic Preservation, and how have the Trust's own programs evolved over the years as it has grown organizationally?*

A. The National Trust for Historic Preservation in the United States is a private, non-profit, charitable and educational organization. It is a membership organization, with over 250,000 members throughout the United States. [We also accept members from foreign countries, and I should go on the record in urging you to join. This sort of public relations pitch is something that you ought to get used to doing: if you end up working for a private organization that is based on membership, get used to the idea of asking people to become members and explaining what your organization does!] The mission of the Trust (which is printed on the bottom of its letterhead so that everyone knows exactly what it is) is to foster an appreciation of the diverse character and meaning of American cultural heritage and to preserve and revitalize the livability of our communities by leading the nation in saving America's historic environments.

The Trust was chartered by Congress in 1949, between the time of the enactment of the Historic Sites Act and the National Historic Preservation Act. The Trust was given a charter at that time to encourage public participation in historic preservation in the United States, because of the feeling that the federal government was unable to respond quickly to preservation issues — and to try to protect significant properties.

There was also a feeling that individuals who owned significant historic properties were unwilling to leave them in their wills (or donate them in their lifetimes) to the federal government because they did not trust or like the federal government. The Trust was therefore also created as a vehicle to accept bequests and donations of historic properties and to maintain them.

The idea at that time was that these would be museum properties; the Trust currently owns eighteen museum properties. Later, the Trust began to focus its activities more on encouraging other organizations and the private sector to undertake preservation activities on their own.

Where does the money come from? The Trust continues to receive a portion of its budget as a grant from the federal government; last year, it received some $7 million out of an annual budget of about $32 million — in other words, less than a quarter of the budget comes from the federal government. The remaining amounts in the budget come from membership fees, royalty income (from items sold), shop income, special events income and endowment income. Of the properties owned and maintained as museums, most have individual endowments that were established to provide funding for their ongoing operation. The Trust also has an endowment to assist in its operations; unfortunately, it does not begin to cover the cost of operations.

Part III:

Controls in the Private Sector

The Balance between Public Regulations and Private Rights

Carsten Lund*

Responsibility

In Denmark, the Division of Cultural Heritage Protection has the responsibility for protecting about 32 percent of the protected and listed ancient monuments; there are also about 100,000 unlisted ancient monuments that are dealt with by the museums in Denmark. Of those monuments, about 22,000 are burial mounds, mainly from the Bronze Age. The 10,000 others could be passage graves, fortifications, ruins (mainly medieval), runic stones, canals and a lot of other remaining structures in the landscape. The cultural landscape is also part of the responsibility of this division in the Danish forest and nature agency.

Other agencies

There are other divisions entirely devoted to protecting landscape or to protecting buildings or urbanized areas.

Links with nature and planning

As an agency of the Ministry of Environment, this agency naturally emphasizes the interaction between nature and culture. That has meant that it has linked the protection of cultural heritage to the regulation of land use for urbanization, industry, infrastructure and agriculture. Denmark has these links in its legislation and in its administration. The agency has to scrutinize all the development plans on which decisions will have to be taken by municipalities, regional councils or the State.

Property rights defined

Property rights belong to the owner and normally include the right of disposal — he/she can buy or sell the protected or unprotected heritage. In Denmark it is easier to get a good price if the property is unprotected than if it is protected.

"Usus, fructus, abusus"

The property is "capital," for the owner to use; the owner has a right to use it in a way that he/she deems best — to cultivate land, to extract minerals, to plant trees, to invite or forbid people to walk on this land, and so forth.

---

* Carsten Lund is a lawyer and head of the Division of Cultural Heritage Protection, which is part of the State agency for protection of forests and nature in the Danish Ministry of Environment.

71

Property rights (for example, in the case of movable objects) include the right to destroy. If the owner does not want this movable heritage any longer, he/she can destroy it. (Some problems concern the rights of artists; for example, the owner of a portrait may not always be allowed to paint a moustache on a painting.)

Grounds for intervention

With movable objects, the regulation and content of ownership rights are fairly easy to understand. It may be more difficult with immovable property, i.e., land, buildings and cultural heritage structures in the landscape such as boundary stone walls, traces of old field systems and road systems. How can the owner use them? The owner may want to destroy the features that the agency and the public want to protect. The problem here is that we have to think of public regulation as a set of ways to interfere with these property rights (the rights of the owner) on a sliding scale

Keystone:
Sliding scale

- from very mild regulation at one end of the scale
- to expropriation at the other end.

The mildest regulation (on one end) and expropriation (on the other) are the outer limits of a scale of interventions by public authorities affecting the rights of the owners.

One end of the spectrum

Expropriation is the absolute. The State takes over all the rights of the owner (that is one of the interesting things about expropriation) and after expropriation, the State can act just as freely as the former owner could.

Unusual measure

In some countries, expropriation is a bad word: they do not like to use it because it suggests a system where private ownership is threatened. European countries have a system in which private ownership is the rule and public ownership is the exception.

Other end of spectrum

Although expropriation is a situation where the State takes over all the rights of the owner, regulation covers all other measures that have an influence directly or indirectly on the rights of the owner. Public regulation of the immovable heritage property can be very mild; it can even take the form of regulation through incentives (which are also a sort of regulation, namely to try to get people to act in a special way by incentives such as grants and tax deductions).

Constitutional conflicts

But regulation can also be very intensive, and thus, we run into a constitutional problem in most countries. Most countries have a preference in their constitutions for private ownership. This has several consequences.

- There are limits to what the State can do, even with legislation and regulation, before it crosses into expropriation.
- There are also in many constitutions limits to the purposes for which the State can expropriate.

- If those limits are crossed, it amounts to expropriation, which can be implemented only when a strong public interest makes it necessary to take over the rights of the owner.
- Often, in such cases, a special procedure must be undertaken, and in many countries, this means going to court.

Scandinavian
situation

The Scandinavian countries have constitutions building upon general European ideas of preference for private ownership, but the Scandinavian countries also accept a very intensive engagement of the public administration in how to treat both the cultural heritage and many other sectors of society. There is also political back-up for rather intensive regulation of owners' rights.

Criteria

Four questions help clarify when an agency crosses the threshold between regulation and expropriation:

1. "Generality": Is the law one of general application or specific to the property?
2. "Actuality": Does the law change behaviour now or only in the future?
3. "Extinction": Does the law extinguish rights or transfer them?
4. "Residual Rights": Does the law leave the owner with any rights?

**1. Laws of
General
Application**

The generality (i.e., generic extent) of the regulation: there is a problem if the regulation contributes to the extinction or transfer of rights. In the Nordic countries, general regulations are not considered to be expropriation if all owners (or at least all owners of property of a certain kind) are subject to the regulation.

Examples

General
application

- In Denmark, all owners of forest lands are obliged to plant trees whenever they cut down trees. That is a regulation; it is not expropriation. All owners of meadows are forbidden to change their use (e.g., they cannot plough them or grow corn on them). This is forbidden by the law on nature protection. Since *all* owners of meadows have this obligation (i.e., "generality"), it is not considered to amount to expropriation (however, the landowners' society has threatened to take this regulation to court since it was passed in 1992 and is "still thinking" about the possibility, but I do not think they will do so).

Identification
of *genus*

- Another example is that all owners of buildings built before 1536 will have to consider that their buildings are automatically protected by a preservation of buildings act (1536 is when the Reformation took place in Denmark; buildings were taken from the Catholic church, and only some of them were used by the Protestant church). On the other hand, instead of regulating all landowners' rights (or at least of all owners of a specific kind of land), a government could have very specific or concrete regulations that affect only one owner (or a few owners). Laws might allow the administration to decide on protection - and not in every case.

2. Present vs. Future

The actuality (as opposed to "potentiality") refers to a situation in which we are regulating an activity that is on-going at the time of the regulation, as opposed to a future possible use of the land.

Effect on listing

In Denmark and in most European countries, the protection of buildings is mainly based on a listing of buildings, where an agency considers each building and decides whether the building should be protected. That is a very concrete regulation of the owner's rights. The agency takes into account only this owner's building and says, "You have to apply for any alterations that you want to make in the future; you will have to keep your building water-tight and maintain it in a reasonable way." That is an example of a very concrete regulation, and yet in Denmark it is not considered an expropriation. Why not?

Criterion: Change of behaviour

- Is it "lack of intensity"? No, that is not the case with the protection of buildings.
- Is it "lack of actuality"? Yes, indeed; the agency is not actually saying to the owner, "You cannot use a building in the way you use it today; you have to change something." The agency is not imposing a change of behaviour, i.e., some change in the use of the property. The actuality of the regulation is missing.

Examples

The Home Rule government of Greenland has a provision that says that if, at the time the agency protects a building it also imposes a specific action on the owner, this is considered to amount to expropriation - and the government has to pay compensation for that imposition.

In Denmark itself, by contrast, the agency does not have the power to impose an action on the building's owner when it is protected, so the agency does not have to pay compensation to the owner when the decision is taken. These are the problems with actuality.

Ultimatum

Often, a proposal to protect a specific building is made when a demolition is imminent. That gives agencies problems, because they cannot really say, "It is not a general regulation." It is a regulation with a very actual application. The approach in Danish legislation and elsewhere (in the Scandinavian laws, at least) is as follows: if an owner of a protected house applies for permission to demolish, and this application is denied, then the owner can demand that it be expropriated. It is in the owner's power to ask the State to take over the property when he/she is not allowed to demolish it, even if it is a protected building. In short, the owner has a right to ask for demolition, but if the request is turned down, the State will have to take over the property. That is why we sometimes see in Denmark some highly interesting buildings that are not protected. It was decided not to protect them because the agency could not have found a proper use for them after the State has taken them over.

Use

The Danish legislation stipulates that protected buildings must be given a function appropriate to the special character of the buildings in order to ensure their preservation in the long term. The best way to protect a building is for the building to have a function that provides a cash flow that can pay for its maintenance. If it does not have that, it will be difficult to maintain over the long term.

Problematic situations

Many countries have special types of buildings that are difficult to preserve. Large industrial installations, as well as churches, are some notable examples of the most difficult. Holland has examples of how churches have been turned into flats or a department store. Such uses were not what we had anticipated with the notion of "appropriate use" for buildings.

Another example of a problematic situation regarding general regulation is the Swedish approach to the protected zone around archaeological monuments. There, the authority has discretion to decide whether the protection zone should extend to 10 metres, 50 metres or even 100 metres. Denmark has a general 100-metre protection zone, but Sweden decides each case individually. Again, it is the lack of actuality in the regulation's interference with the owner's rights that means that it is not deemed to be expropriation, and as a result, the agency does not have to pay compensation.

3. Extinction vs. Transfer

The next dimension is the principle of extinction versus transfer of rights.

- What is meant by extinction or transfer of rights?
- If one extinguishes the rights, they do not exist any more for anyone; but
- if one transfers them, it is another person (or juridical person such as the State or other authority) who can exercise these rights.

So if one just extinguishes the rights, it is like saying that "all landowners do not have this right any more - because nobody has this right any more." That is extinction of rights.

One example of extinction is our law for the protection of nature, which allows the public to have access to privately owned forests for recreation such as walking. That is a general provision, but there is an exception saying that the owner is entitled to close specific parts of the forest for a specific reason, although the regional council can overrule the owner's decision. This situation is, in the first place, an extinction of owner's rights, but when the exception is applied, the situation changes and the owner still maintains some rights. However, even those rights can be overruled by authorities in the end. That is again an extinction of rights, i.e., the owner's right to forbid people to walk on the land.

Why is this action not deemed to be an expropriation? Apparently, it is considered to "lack intensity." But some owners have strong feelings indeed about other people walking on their land: they feel that this legislative situation has very intensive effects. A threat from landowners' associations that they may take this matter to court has so far not been put into action.

A different example is that of an archaeological investigation on private land, where the government decides to restore a monument, open it to the public and build a visitor centre on this area: this is an expropriation. Is that different from the example of visitors in the forest? Why is one an expropriation and not the other? The answer (as best as one can make out) is that in the latter case, there has been a *transfer* of the right of the owner (to do whatever he/she wants) to the public service — that is, to build a visitor centre to show the area to the public. Admittedly, in practice, it can be difficult to see the difference between these examples.

4. Residual Rights

Regulation can deal with a number of the owner's rights, but if only very few rights are left, the situation will often be considered "expropriation."

That raises some difficult questions in the context of heritage designations in Denmark. For example,

- the designation of a house as a protected house means that all alterations of both the exterior and the interior will have to be scrutinized (by the forest and nature agency); furthermore,
- if the agency turns down an application for alteration, the owners cannot carry it out — and have nowhere to go to have this decision overruled.

Ultimate recourse

That is a very intensive regulation, but why is it not considered an expropriation? The answer is that the owners are left with the possibility of asking for the demolition of the building if they cannot live with the rejection of their application for alteration. Then they can say, "We have to live with it, but if we cannot live with it, we will ask for demolition of the building." That would then provoke an expropriation procedure.

Another example is the designation or listing of an archaeological monument, where the owner cannot really make any alterations: the owner is allowed to apply for a licence to alter an archaeological monument but, realistically, will never get the licence to do so. That is a very intensive regulation, but why is it not labelled an expropriation? The answer is that normally, the designation is done when the owner has no intention of doing any specific work anyway, so the actuality is not very high, and what is then left for the owner to do? Furthermore, what can the owner still do with an archaeological monument on the land? He/she can still cut down wood that is on the archaeological monument but must abide by any regulation allowing the regional council to enter the land and cut down wood if it thinks that the monument looks better without the trees than with the trees; the council cannot walk off with the wood, however, because it remains the owner's property. So this is a very intensive regulation.

The residual rights of the owner were revealed in a rather funny case several years ago. A former professor of archaeology was turning seventy years old and was about to retire, so some of his friends wanted to give him a birthday present. They bought an ancient monument situated in a field in Denmark, a nice stone with a mask on it from the Bronze Age. They turned over the deed to this stone to the professor. A couple of months later, the professor received a letter from the landowner saying, "You have a stone lying on my ground. Would you please take it away because it is disturbing my use of the land."

The professor asked us, "What can I do with this? I cannot move it, because that would be in violation of the protection of ancient monuments."

We had to tell him, "Yes, that's true. You cannot move it from the land, so you had better buy the land from the landowner, because otherwise he can charge you rent for having your monument lying on his land."

That is one of the extreme stories that a country sometimes runs into with the very few rights that are left for the owner of an archaeological monument.

Returning to one of the four principles — actuality — here are two crucial points:

Change may force expropriation

- Regulations can forbid future changes of the use of the land or of the use of a building (or future changes to a building), but
- it cannot force the owner to change the current use. If the agency does that, then it has crossed the line into expropriation.

Therefore, if an agency wants an immediate change anywhere, it will have to expropriate. Denmark's agency does not always use that phrase; it can also use different tools (called conservation easements or conservation decisions with compensation), or it can buy the property from the owner; then it is not regulating, it is buying. If it wants to have a transfer of rights, to act very intensively or to introduce a specific regulation towards one piece of property, then it can either buy or it can expropriate (with the different tools of expropriation under different names).

Examples

Two examples of actuality are the protection of ancient monuments and of archaeological sites.

- When archaeological sites are not under agricultural cultivation, Denmark's agency protects them only if they are listed monuments;
- if they are under the surface of a cultivated field, they are not listed as protected monuments. Instead, they are protected in another way: the State Antiquarian has the right to enter, conduct an archaeological excavation, move out again, take away all the finds, store them in museums and document the excavation. That is the way these resources would be preserved for the future, i.e., as finds and documentation.

Therefore, if the agency wants to protect them as monuments instead, it either has to act when they are not under actual agricultural cultivation, or to expropriate them (as explained) and pay compensation to the owner, who would have no right to cultivate this area with the monument on it.

An example at the other end of the scale is physical planning for the protection of cultural heritage. That means forbidding future changes of the use or appearance of the site. A problem often arises when a rescue operation is carried out on an archaeological find, and authorities discover that it is too important for straight excavation. Here is the argument: "Why should the archaeologists of today make all the mistakes? Let's keep some of it *in situ* for future archaeologists to make their mistakes, too." So we have to protect the archaeological monuments against even the archaeologists. And if the agency agrees with that argument, it then has to step over the limit and conduct expropriations.

Interaction

Although these four principles are outlined in order to make some distinctions in the regulation of private property, they interact. All four are always there in some way or other, and they act together simultaneously.

Criteria
summarized

Public legal regulation as a means of protecting cultural heritage should never stand alone because an agency can

- use it only to a certain intensity;
- use it in certain cases of not very imminent changes;
- use it when it is of fairly general application, and

- use it when it does not transfer too many of the owner's rights to the public state or authority.

Economic support

Legal regulation should not stand alone. It should always be accompanied by economic measures, such as the deductible depreciation to cover decay per year. This is a notion that, in Denmark, has been developed by the Association of Owners of Protected Buildings. They have developed a system that says: "This part of a building will normally last as long as thirty years, this other part should be maintained every fifth year, and this other part of a building can last for fifty years, etc." When they look at a protected building for which assistance has been sought, they help to calculate the decay per year, and the owner is allowed, under Danish tax legislation, a deduction for decay per year.

Depreciation tailored to life-cycle costing

In other words, the owners do not need to have undertaken actual maintenance work in a given year at a given magnitude. The owner can deduct through the years the theoretical decay per year and put the tax savings into a bank account, so that when maintenance is needed, this money can be withdrawn and used.

Other supportive measures

There are also other economic incentives, such as freedom from property tax, that apply in Denmark for protected buildings. Other features have made the situation in Denmark so favourable for owners of protected buildings that now we have owners coming to the agency asking the agency to declare a building a protected building in order to benefit from these incentives.

Property tax

Consulting service

There are other possibilities, i.e.,

- reduction of inheritance tax,
- grants or subsidies, or
- free consultant advice to people, a measure that is particularly important. People are advised on how to maintain their historic property or are advanced the money to hire a good architect who understands the business and who knows the importance of a building (the agency also wants to encourage the market for good architects in the historic buildings area).

Legal safety net

On the other hand, we must accept that it is necessary to have basic public legal regulation. This is recognized all over Europe, and it is also recognized in the *European Convention for the Protection of the Architectural Heritage of Europe* (the Council of Europe's convention) as well as the new *European Convention for the Protection of the Archaeological Heritage of Europe*. These two conventions require states to have a minimum level of public regulation, i.e., legal regulation, to secure the protected monuments.

The path of the future?

In Denmark, public regulations have developed more and more intensely and with a high degree of general application.

79

We Danes are very aware of that generality, and simultaneously we are moving along the line of intensity. One example is drawn from the area of nature protection, which has moved furthest along this line: e.g., all lakes in Denmark that have a surface larger than 100 square metres are protected and cannot be changed. A pond that is the size of the conference room at Smolenice Castle would be a protected lake in Denmark. Another example is that of meadows (or uncultivated grassland) of more than 2,500 square metres: these too are protected. That is the size of a large garden, which causes tremendous problems to the bureaucracy because it already has to process an immense number of applications for changes. That is one of the pragmatic problems when an agency moves to increasingly intense general regulation. It has to set up an administration (bureaucracy) to follow up on such regulation.

On the other hand, that could become a means of protection in itself — "protection through bureaucratization" (it is one of the nice notions that we have worked very hard on in Denmark). The generality here keeps us out of the problem of expropriation but makes it more difficult to have sympathetic attitudes to landowners' views regarding nature protection. Although some years ago nature protection was very popular, even with landowners, Denmark now faces a problem with landowners who are less interested in it.

Public support

The cultural protection legislation has kept farther away from generality, i.e., closer to designation procedures where the agency protects (not generically but more specifically) each monument individually. Admittedly, that brings this agency closer to expropriating, but it makes it easier for it to explain what it does and why, which helps the public, and even landowners, to have a more sympathetic attitude towards the protection of cultural heritage. In fact, in Denmark there is a very sympathetic attitude — even among landowners — which helps the agency and makes it less necessary to use fines or other strong methods of enforcement. It would be very difficult to implement and enforce public regulations that are not considered by the public at large to be in accordance with the public's interests as defined by ordinary people.

Legislation is not the only source for regulating behaviour of people. It may not even be the most important source. People are also tempted by other things (or deterred by other things) than legislation. The conservation community will have to focus more on raising awareness. After all, the heritage is the people's heritage.

Participants' Questions

Q. *America has been experiencing tremendous change in the attitudes property owners have towards landmarking. Has there been a change in the attitudes of European property owners lately?*

A. They are louder now than during the 1970s. During the last ten years, landowners have become more aware of the increasing regulation they face. However, regulation from the heritage branch is nothing compared to what agricultural producers face from Brussels in the European Union. For example, there's a well-organized system of consultants who can tell the farmer what is advisable to grow this year, but it might be totally different next year — and there are penalties for overproduction. Cumulatively, any regulation is now perceived as a nuisance, even if it is in a sympathetic field such as cultural heritage. The total amount of regulation has not made it easier for us to explain why people should abide by rules on cultural heritage protection.

Here is another example of rules from Brussels that do not further the protection of cultural heritage. In order to reduce fishing levels within the Union, they have set up a system of grants for destroying fishing boats (they pay 70 percent of the replacement insurance value). When the fisherman wants to get out of business, he gets 70 percent of his boat's value if he destroys it. Ironically, the ones who want to get out of fishing are often the ones who own the most interesting examples of cultural heritage vessels. We have to compete with 70 percent grants from Brussels to demolish cultural heritage! That is not easy.

Q. *Let us suppose that I owned a building in Denmark. Instead of having an official knocking at my door saying "Keep your hands off that monument unless we tell you," is it possible that I would ever have an official knocking at my door saying, "You lucky person, you don't realize what a magnificent building you have, and we will show you how you can do it properly"?*

A. Yes, in fact, both persons are in the same agency. Often, people want to make a change — they want a new bathroom or to rearrange the rooms in a listed building — so they turn to the authority, which says: "Yes, this is a complicated project that you have taken on. We will help you, we will provide financing to hire a consultant who knows about these problems and who knows about that type of house, we will pay the professional fee to help you find the right solution." A private consulting architect provides this advice.

Q. *When an owner wishes to either demolish or alter the building, your government doesn't reply, "There is a perfectly reasonable use for your building." Your government can be forced to acquire the building even though there would be a reasonable use. Your government would then turn it over to somebody* *else. Is that how it works? We are used (in the United States) to a system where, if a person asks to alter or demolish, there is then an opportunity for the government to show that the owner can make a reasonable return without that inappropriate alteration (or without that demolition). It is only if that second test fails that the government can be forced to the expropriation payment. Are you missing that middle phase?*

A. The owner's application to demolish is dealt with like any other application. If we can convince the owner that it is not necessary because the owner can still do this or that, of course we will try to do it. But if the owner insists on demolition, we in Denmark have to say either yes or no. And if we say no, the owner has the right to ask for public expropriation, for the State to take over the property, and to be paid a compensation for the market value for that property.

ADDENDUM (Lisbeth Saaby)

In Denmark, if an owner of a listed building wants to alter or demolish it, the owner asks for consent at the national agency. A procedure then starts, in which negotiations with the owner are essential elements. During those negotiations, the agency (or the consulting expert who has been asked to help in these negotiations) might suggest new uses, show that this house can be used appropriately, or suggest new functions, in order to explain to the owner that there is no need for demolition or for this objectionable alteration. But it is not a must: it is often an assessment of the concrete circumstances of the demand presented by the owner. There are no provisions telling the agency that it has to discuss an appropriate use or function with the owner (in order to tell him that it can be feasible or viable).

Q. *What techniques or schemes might be appropriate for raising awareness in the community or among the current administrators, particularly in Central and Eastern Europe?*

A. Denmark has a system for architectural evaluation called the SAVE system: the agency provides economic help for municipalities and local groups to evaluate their built heritage. It starts with a local public hearing, where the municipal council and all the different local associations that have an interest in the field of cultural heritage are invited. After this hearing, a local group is formed to evaluate the built heritage in the area and general needs for protection. After the group has worked with a strict methodology prescribed by the agency, in close consultation with the local people, it produces an attractive publication — which the mayor, incidentally, is usually eager to present to visitors. After the publication, the local group is encouraged to scrutinize all the local (physical) planning, to identify where prospective actions or threats to cultural heritage.

This approach has succeeded in raising public awareness of local cultural heritage in many areas, but it is expensive, because you work with one area at a time. We have 275 municipalities in Denmark, so it will take us some years to get around to all of them.

Q. *Does Denmark offer only two possibilities — excavation (i.e., destruction) at an archaeological site or expropriation?*

A. You could imagine solutions other than to excavate or to expropriate: I have made some simplifications during my presentation. We have a lot of other tools – for example, we can give a grant to the landowner to take a field out of production and have permanent grass over the area. We can buy the land. We can negotiate with the owner to make sure that the archaeological heritage is not further destroyed.

Q. *Can owners in Denmark propose that their property become a monument? If so, what organization rules on this proposal?*

A. Owners have indeed done so — in larger numbers recently, because of the incentives attached to possible protection. The proposal would reviewed by the agency and a central board for protection of buildings (consisting of art historians, architects, representatives of owners of protected buildings, etc.).

Regulation in a
Complex Constitutional Setting:
United States Case Study

*Stephen Neal Dennis**

United States
background

The following is a description of two phenomena:

a) how the legal system in the United States developed its approach to historic preservation (over a historical period of perhaps ninety years) and

b) how the U.S. land-use regulation system evolved to the point where it is today.

Choice of
government leve

One frequently asked question is whether historic preservation regulatory controls are better imposed at the national level or at a local or regional level. The United States, in effect, does it both ways.

How the United States has developed a bifurcated (or what is perhaps now becoming tri-furcated) system requires historical explanation.

Original
position

In the United States, "property rights" are protected by the constitution. In the nineteenth century, there were basically no land-use regulatory controls in the United States, except those that developed under nuisance law: citizens were not supposed to use their property in such a way that it became obnoxious to nearby property owners. As an example, an owner should not have a pig farm in the middle of an entirely residential neighbourhood.

Height controls
introduced
and tested in
Boston

At the turn of the century, Boston had a height ordinance (i.e., a municipal decree) that restricted the number of floors a building could have. The constitutional legality of that ordinance was challenged in court. The case went to our highest court, the United States Supreme Court, which upheld the

* Stephen Neal Dennis is a lawyer in Washington, D.C., and Past Executive Director of the U.S. National Center for Preservation Law.

Boston ordinance and therefore allowed cities to impose height restrictions.

Set-back controls in New York

Then in 1916, New York became concerned that skyscrapers were becoming too tall. There was fear that a great concentration of tall buildings in a small urban area would mean that people working and living on the streets far below would have very little light and would not have clean air to breathe. New York therefore created something unprecedented, which it called a "Zoning Resolution." It required tall buildings to have set-backs at various levels; a building might go up, say, fifteen storeys and then the building would have to become smaller. It might rise another seven storeys and then become smaller again. This was an effort to let light penetrate to the streets far below. As news of New York's innovative procedure spread around the country, other cities tried their own approaches to a zoning scheme.

Opposition in court

These early schemes were extremely controversial. They were quickly tested in court cases, and state courts were about evenly divided by the early 1920s; half of the state courts that had heard these cases thought that zoning regulations were appropriate, while the other half of the state courts thought that they were dubious and perhaps "unconstitutional" (as being contrary to the U.S.A.'s protection of "property rights"). Inevitably, a case developed that would again go to the United States Supreme Court, which ruled in 1926 (in a case called *Euclid v. Ambler*) that a zoning classification scheme (which had separated a small city into a residential area, an industrial area and a commercial area) was valid from a constitutional standpoint.

Segregation of uses

This led to an approach to zoning that Americans called "Euclidian" (based on the name of the case, not on Euclidian geometry), namely that land uses should be strictly separated to prevent mixed-use neighbourhoods. That philosophy is now being questioned by many planners who believe that downtown cities are perhaps healthier if there is a mixture of uses (e.g., so that commercial uses and residential uses can occupy the same district).

In the United States, land-use regulation has historically been a matter for

- legislative authorization at the state level (on whether to allow municipalities to act in this area), and
- legislative implementation at the local level.

Dissemination of "models"

Accordingly, when the U.S. federal Department of Commerce became interested in this zoning (as a philosophical approach) in the 1920s, it developed two model pieces of recommended legislation:

- one was a model state statute;
- the other was a model municipal ordinance.

Extension to
historic
preservation

Not surprisingly, after the 1926 Supreme Court decision in the <u>Euclid</u> case, many communities of all sizes began to think that a zoning approach might be useful to them. Charleston, South Carolina, an older city on the Atlantic coast, with prominent architectural development from the eighteenth and early nineteenth centuries, adopted its first zoning ordinance in 1931, but instead of simply copying the federal Department of Commerce's recommended ordinance, Charleston made an innovation. Charleston added a provision that we would today call a local historic preservation ordinance.

Charleston's
experiment

Charleston had a concern that was not unique, although its approach was visionary. A number of American museums and wealthy private collectors had begun buying significant architectural woodwork in the 1920s; they would buy entire rooms of eighteenth-century panelling or staircases, doors, windows — whatever they thought would be interesting to insert in a new house that they might be building somewhere else. City leaders in Charleston, as well as concerned local architects and community leaders, realized that important buildings were being demolished so that these rooms could be removed and taken from Charleston to other cities. Charleston's intention in adding this provision to its zoning ordinance was to prevent this from happening. It created a Board of Architectural Review with powers to review certain actions by property owners in a defined area of the city. Charleston created an Old and Historic District (initially it was a relatively small area of the city, which is on a peninsula between two rivers). The Board of Architectural Review was empowered to meet monthly, if necessary, and to review applications from owners who wished to alter their buildings, construct new buildings in the historic district or, worst of all, demolish an existing building.

Charleston's Board was extremely successful. The area regulated by the Board has been expanded several times, most significantly in the 1960s. Perhaps the greatest tribute to the effectiveness of the Board is the fact that its powers were never challenged in court until the 1970s. It operated for almost forty-five years before any local property owner decided to argue in court that the Board's powers might be somehow limited.

Charleston was
copied...slowly

Other cities began to copy this approach. New Orleans enacted an ordinance in 1936. San Antonio, Texas, which has many early Spanish-style buildings, passed an ordinance in 1939. Alexandria, Virginia, acted in 1946. But nationwide, this process developed very slowly in the beginning. It was one city here, one city there. There was in no sense a national movement.

Then, in the 1950s, after some court cases from New Orleans, the United States finally saw the introduction of state enabling legislation; at first, legislation would simply authorize a given city here or there to pass such an ordinance. Then there followed several state-wide laws to authorize any city within a particular state to enact such legislation.

In our country, the federal government does not enact land-use regulation provisions. This power is essentially possessed at the state level and then delegated (in one way or another) to local governments. Local governments therefore have enormous land-use regulation power. Furthermore, even though state zoning statutes may be quite similar from state to state, on the topic of historic preservation there has been great variety and experimentation.

It was not until 1955 that Philadelphia, Pennsylvania, enacted the first truly city-wide historic preservation ordinance. All the earlier ordinances had dealt with small areas in a single city but never with an entire city. Philadelphia's ordinance, though, not only dealt with the entire large city of Philadelphia, but also introduced a new concept, namely that of landmarks, which are not exactly synonymous with monuments (as will become clear later). What the Philadelphia ordinance contemplated was that the City of Philadelphia would pass local ordinances designating individual historic structures as local landmark properties. The local landmarks would then come under the jurisdiction of the Philadelphia Historical Commission. The Commission would carry on survey work to identify buildings eligible for possible designation in the future, but the designation process itself would be done individually (building by building) and might (in some cases) be relatively slow.

In 1966, New York City was the first city in the United States to have a city-wide ordinance that allowed both

- historic districts, and
- individual landmark structures.

The British term "conservation area" is very similar to the U.S. term "historic district." The idea is that both historic and non-historic structures within the boundaries of the historic district are regulated, so that there are no unsympathetic alterations that damage the appearance and fabric of the historic district. Over time, as inevitable changes do occur, the character of the district can be maintained and even in some cases enhanced as non-contributing buildings are gradually eliminated.

From 1931 until 1966 this concept of the local historic preservation ordinance really developed. In the 1970s the number of cities with such ordinances increased very dramatically.

Although in 1955 there had been perhaps only 20 such cities in the entire country, and in 1965 there were still only about 100, in 1975, there were at least 500. There are today close to 2,000. The growth has been rapid and dramatic.

There are now so many of these commissions in every state across the country that there is a single national non-profit charitable organization called the National Alliance of Preservation Commissions. Its entire purpose is to develop information that will help the members of these local preservation commissions do a better job of exercising their responsibilities and overseeing the historic properties that come within their jurisdiction.

At the same time (and quite independently), the U.S.A.'s national program (or "federal program," as it is called) had been developing, but the national government's involvement in historic preservation came relatively slowly. About thirty years after the American Civil War (that is, in the early 1890s), as soldiers who

had been young men in the 1860s were getting older, there was a movement to memorialize the war by creating some national battlefield monuments. A court case in 1895 addressed the question of whether the federal government could legally purchase property for such a purpose, if an owner was not otherwise willing to sell. That court case, involving the Gettysburg Battlefield in Pennsylvania, held that the federal government did have the power to expropriate property for such a purpose and to pay the owner of the property.

Then came the Antiquities Act (1906) and the Historic Sites Act (1935), which created two important federal programs that ultimately proved to be somewhat ineffective. The first was the National Historic Landmarks Program to identify our most important proper-

ties and allow them to be recognized as such through an official national classification as a landmark. However, there is an essential caveat here. Federal designation for National Historic Landmark purposes is not at all the same as local land-use designation for landmark purposes:

- The federal classification carries with it no regulations that restrict the actions of the private landowner. The way the program has developed is that the federal government will now try to reach an agreement with the private owner so that, in return for the landmark designation, the owner will agree to undertake certain responsibilities to maintain the building.

- As for land-use regulation that prevents alteration, incompatible new construction or demolition, those controls are essentially at the local level.

A second program was created in 1935, namely the Historic American Buildings Survey (HABS). This was an attempt to photograph historic buildings and to develop (for archival purposes) a system of measured drawings. In the early days of the program, some buildings had both measured drawings and photographs; other buildings (where the program was more embryonic) had only photographs.

Perceived failure

By 1964, however, people discovered that one-third of the buildings recorded under this program had already been demolished or badly altered. It was clearly a program that was not protecting buildings, although it was recognizing their importance. A group of American leaders sponsored by the Council of Mayors came to Europe for one summer to study European historic preservation programs. They went back to the United States and developed a piece of federal legislation called the National Historic Preservation Act, which was enacted by Congress in 1966. The "National Register of Historic Places" was created, which was to be different from the National Historic Landmarks Program.

National Register

The old Landmarks Program at the federal level had been designed to recognize only the most important buildings — "*la crème de la crème*." The National Register Program, however, was designed to recognize buildings important at the national level or the state level or a purely local level.

Incorrect level for private regulation

In the United States, this has led to much confusion in terminology because under the National Register program, it is possible to have historic districts, as well as individually listed properties. And non-professionals in many communities are often confused about whether they have a *local* historic district or a *National Register* historic district. This confusion is unfortunate because as far as restrictions on a private owner, there are essentially none from a National Register listing. It is honorific. It is a program designed to help federal agencies in their planning of federal projects but the National Register program, which identifies and recognizes historic properties, does not impede or restrict actions by private owners. It is *local* designation as a landmark or inclusion in a local historic district which has that potential.

Two levels with different effects

This is how the United States found itself with a bifurcated system:

- At the level of the national government, the country has a program to survey, identify and designate properties — the

National Register of Historic Places. Once listed, a property receives much publicity. The publicity can have a valuable impact on the owner for it confirms that his/her building is important and should be maintained, but a national listing does not force an owner to do anything or prevent him/her from doing anything.

- At the level of the local governments, there are local listings that have the capability of compelling or deterring private owners.

Third level
similar to
national

The United States is beginning to have, however, a third system at the intermediate or state level. Many states are developing their own state registers of historic places, which again are designed as a planning tool to guide state agencies in their implementation of various projects they may be wishing to undertake.

Link to
incentives

In the background are financial and tax incentives that vary greatly from state to state. In some states they are keyed to or triggered by a listing in a state register of historic properties. In other states, they may be keyed to or triggered by a listing on the National Register of Historic Places, and sometimes there is a requirement of local listing.

Layering

It is possible, in certain states, for a single property to be listed on three different registers of historic properties:

- it might be formally listed on the National Register of Historic Places,
- it might be listed in a state register of historic properties, and
- it might be locally designated or included within a local historic district.

Within the United States' own legal system, however, it is always the local designation that has the greatest impact on property owners who would wish to alter or damage historic properties.

Results

I do not believe that one hundred years ago, anyone in our country trying to think ahead and to project how historic properties might be protected today could possibly have predicted a system such as the one we have developed.

In a sense, the system as it has developed within the United States has sometimes been accidental, haphazard and unintended. Unless one follows the historical development (from that late nineteenth-century interest in having the federal government acquire certain key historic properties, to today), it is difficult to make sense of this development.

Other
conclusions

Something that has also taken place within the popular mind is a growing appreciation of a fundamental point:

- It is not just single historic properties with great historical or patriotic importance that need to be protected,
- it is entire neighbourhoods, scenic landscapes, archaeological sites, etc., that are even more important in many communities.

Comparison with past

In the middle of the nineteenth century, there was great concern about sites where George Washington had camped during the American Revolutionary War, or about the homes of founding fathers. At the time of the Civil War, a group of women acquired Mount Vernon, the home of George Washington, believing it was a site that must be protected. As an example of how curious the approach to historic preservation was at that time, a famous Philadelphia architect suggested in the 1870s that to "preserve" Mount Vernon, it should be rebuilt entirely in white marble (which would make it "everlasting"). It is, in fact, a relatively simple frame building. To have rebuilt it in white marble would have been to entirely transform it — and yet that was one approach to dealing with a major historic building following the Civil War.

Not surprisingly, this multi-level governmental set-up can be confusing. In response to the frequent international question of whether it is better to have historic preservation controls at the national level or at the local level, it may not be possible to provide a firm answer except that in the United States' situation, it finds the most effective controls are those at the local level. Those controls, though, are generally administered by volunteer members of local preservation commissions.

Choice of approaches

- There is usually an architect on such a commission, a historian, someone who is active in the real estate community, and often a lawyer.
- These commissions typically range in size from five to nine members.
- They may have paid staff. Often, though, they have no paid staff, so decisions affecting the plans of property owners are made by volunteer commissions.

Where the work is done

- These commissions are usually composed of "amateurs" interested in the cultural resources in the community where they live (but, in larger communities, advised by paid professional staff).

Participants' Questions

Q. *In the United States, historic properties can be designated in three different ways (federal, state, local). Are there relative advantages or disadvantages, or are the underlying interests the same? Is the administration of the preservation interest the same?*

A. No, it is not. In the United States, the protection from private works is local. Furthermore, the level of interest may not be the same. Sometimes, even when three levels of designation are possible, one of the three levels might refuse to designate.

The Chicago Stock Exchange Building, designed by Louis Sullivan, who was one of the United States' greatest late nineteenth-century architects, was never designated by the City of Chicago. It was a building of international significance; the City of Chicago was well aware of that, but simply refused to designate it at the municipal level as a Chicago landmark.

In San Francisco, a department store building called the City of Paris was bought by Neiman Marcus, a chain of specialty stores from Texas. The buyer wanted its site, which was on a downtown square — it was interested in the land but not the City of Paris building. The building had been recognized as a California state landmark and was listed in the National Register of Historic Places. Despite strong arguments, city officials decided they wished to be helpful to Neiman Marcus, so local designation was not made, and the City of Paris building was demolished. There was a compromise of sorts: the great balconied rotunda, rising through the building with an art glass dome on top, was relocated to the outer corner of the new building. This new building, which is faced in diamond-shaped blocks of alternating light and dark stone, has now been voted one of the ugliest buildings in San Francisco by local residents. However, at the time when there was an opportunity to protect the original City of Paris building, those people in the city who had the authority to make the decision were not willing to do it.

The reasons for designation can differ slightly, but generally there is a great deal of overlap. The criteria that would be used for designation at the federal level are often adopted verbatim in local ordinances.

ADDENDUM (Dorothy Miner)

The protective measures that come into play at the different levels are different. Only at the local level is there usually the potential, in the United States, for private action on privately owned property to be fully regulated, if the local law is so enacted. The federal and state reviews will come into play only if there is either federal action, state action or some kind of governmental benefit, like a tax benefit or grant being given. That is the reason for three levels of designation: they complement and supplement each other, but do not duplicate each other.

ADDENDUM (Stephen Dennis)

One reason they are useful is that smaller communities may not be wealthy and may have a difficult time finding the money necessary to hire a qualified architectural historian to do a complete local survey. Much of this survey work has been done by staff from state historic preservation offices, and those offices often operate, in part, with federal historic preservation money.

The United States has, to some extent, a "trickle-down" effect: Congress will appropriate a large amount of money to the National Park Service every year; much of that money then goes to state historic preservation offices, and increasingly, the state offices are making smaller grants to local municipalities that meet certain federal requirements.

However, even when a building is listed in the National Register of Historic Places or has been recognized as a National Historic Landmark, we often lose such buildings. For example, there was a bitterly fought court case about ten years ago involving an entire National Register Historic District in Omaha, Nebraska, composed of large warehouse structures. A wealthy corporation had bought a great deal of land in the vicinity of this historic district and decided that these warehouse buildings were not compatible with their plans. Every single one of the buildings was ultimately demolished. That has been perhaps the most radical example of the inability of the National Register Program (as it operated at that time) to protect a historic district.

Q. *What is the ideal form of ownership for historic properties? Is it State ownership, or private or possibly State ownership with long-term (twenty-year or fifty-year) leases to private owners?*

A. It is impossible to give a consistent answer to that question: so much depends on the identity of the individual building. Many of our governments believe that they have restricted funds and would find it difficult to acquire large numbers of historic properties. Even the U.S. National Park Service is reluctant to acquire additional historic properties, because it means taking on an annual requirement to spend money maintaining the property and paying staff necessary to interpret the property for museum purposes to the public.

We have had great problems at the local level with municipalities: they are sometimes less responsible as owners than private individuals might be. Our worst offenders, however, tend to be large institutions like hospitals, universities or state government complexes. Such institutions have tended to develop long-range schemes without sharing those schemes with the public. Properties will be bought up over a long period of time and then systematically demolished.

For example, one university in the District of Columbia has a small urban campus. It bought perhaps eight or ten square blocks of property. Much of that land has been redeveloped with large office buildings that have some classroom space, but this is primarily office space, and the university treats those buildings as its endowment. Those buildings are designed to produce revenues, which help the university pay its other expenses.

Long-term leases, under the British and American legal systems, include a concept called "waste": the lessee may not violate the terms of the lease, and unless the lease specifically permits demolition, the lessee will be required to return the building at the end of the lease. In London, for instance, where many properties are held on very long-term leases, when a lease comes to an end the lessee is required to return the property to the landlord in good condition. For example, I have a friend who leased a townhouse in London, and she is spending a great deal of money dealing now with dry rot in roof timbers. The problem must be fixed, and the longer the problem is delayed, the more expensive it will be to fix it.

The answer to this question of acquisition and leases varies according to the ownership and the status of the building. In the United States, our governmental units are very reluctant to acquire other buildings. Public ownership, however, is not the only option. The United States and other countries possess a large network of private organizations that are charitable, not governmental, and that own many historic properties. They are able to seek funds from the public or to accept government grants, and they can own and administer a property over a very long period of time. They are often the most effective way of protecting a single property, but again it depends on the resources in a particular community and the nature of the property.

Q. *Within the context of historic preservation, how far should a program of property restitution go from both a political standpoint and a financial standpoint?*

A. There was a conference on privatization several years ago. The approaches to privatization appear to vary greatly from country to country. The problem is that if property is returned or privatized (or, as is said in Poland, "re-privatized"), the new private owner often has no financial resources to spend on the building. If the building is not in good condition at the time of privatization, there is no way for the building to produce an economic return, what is called a "cash flow." The building will not produce money until money is spent on it to repair it.

One possibility, which avoids the concern in some countries about important properties being sold to foreign interests, is to develop a scheme for long-term leases to foreign interests, with a requirement that such foreign interests pay money that could then be spent to restore the properties. Any leasing arrangement would need to be watched carefully, to be certain that money generated by the building is in fact spent to maintain and improve the building.

Q. *If the State owns property, wants privatization, but wants to preserve the property, would it not be a decent idea to sell the property and retain a "conservation easement"?*

A. In countries like the United States, it is possible to acquire a partial interest in a piece of property which we call an "easement." In Civil Code countries, it is called a "servitude." It can be a requirement that an owner do something, or more likely a prohibition against something an owner might otherwise do. We often sell historic properties subject to these servitudes or easements, stating that the owner will not alter or demolish without the consent of a preservation organization or agency.

If there is an active real estate market, this strategy might be very effective. If the private real estate market, however, is only beginning and is very inactive, this strategy might be very slow to accomplish its intended results.

Q. *Doesn't the question of whether such properties should be owned by the State or individuals depend entirely upon the laws that protect the building? For example, in some countries the State can do whatever it wants, whether a building is historic or not; and in other countries if the State owns the property, the property is protected.*

A. My response to the first part of the question would be that if the State owns large numbers of historic properties, it may not matter how much "power" the State has theoretically, if the State itself does not have adequate funds to maintain these historic properties. At a time when there are competing demands on State resources, not everyone will agree that historic conservation is the most important social goal to be accomplished.

It is therefore not simply a question of how much authority this State has, but it is also a question of the economic capability of the State. Some countries will have the funds to maintain large numbers of historic properties. In England, for instance, there are annual governmental grants to an organization called English Heritage, which in turn makes substantial grants to the owners of many historic properties of all sizes across the country. That program has been in place now for a number of years. Other European countries have various kinds of grant programs, but there can be problems. Even in England, one fund that was set up as a memorial to soldiers was raided for other purposes and effectively had to be re-created in the 1970s. In the United States, one federal fund was authorized to exist at a certain size, but Congress has never been willing to appropriate the entire amount or money in any one year. The lesson is that things may look fine in concept or in theory, but political reality may in fact be very different.

ADDENDUM (Thompson Mayes)

It is important for a country, in trying to identify whether continued State ownership is preferable to some form of private ownership, to also look at the use to which the individual property will be put, rather than thinking of it as an across-the-board, generalized policy decision. There are some uses that may encourage the preservation of an individual property in State ownership, and others that may provide internal incentives for preservation in private ownership.

In particular, one situation that occurs often in the United States is where private residences are threatened with demolition. Local people often assume that they should buy the property and turn it into a small museum. That may not be in the best interest of the preservation of the property in the long term — most of the smaller museums in the United States are painfully underfunded. Even though there is a great local commitment (emotionally and philosophically) to the preservation of the property, "deferred maintenance" builds up, and eventually the small preservation group may find that it has a building in need of serious repair and that it has not done an effective job of preserving the property.

Therefore, it is often better for a property to stay in some form of active use where people will continue to invest in its repair and maintenance, rather than to remove it from that use and make it into a museum. Use is an important factor to look at, when trying to identify the appropriate types of ownership.

ADDENDUM (Stephen Dennis)

Some buildings are of such an unusual character that it may be difficult to decide what an appropriate use might be. In Philadelphia, for example, there is an early nineteenth-century prison called Eastern Penitentiary. Its design was innovative at the time of its construction; there were long wings of prison cells radiating from a central core, like the spokes of a wheel, to make it easier for the prison guards to watch the prisoners. It has been archaic for prison use for many years, and the preservation community in Philadelphia has been struggling with the question of appropriate new uses for this large, solidly constructed but extremely deteriorated structure. Despite many suggestions, some buildings are of such an unusual character that when their original function ceases, it is very difficult to design a new function.

Pittsburgh has another set of examples, namely steel mills from the turn of the century. Many have now ceased to operate, but it is difficult to convert them to another industrial use. It may be possible to have one or two industrial museums in such facilities, but no more than one or two in the same community — even a community with as much private philanthropic wealth as Pittsburgh has.

ADDENDUM (Lisbeth Saaby)

On the question of State ownership versus private ownership, one part of Denmark had some experience in that respect, namely Greenland. Before Home Rule was introduced, all old buildings were owned by the State (Denmark); with Home Rule it was envisaged that those buildings should be acquired by the municipalities or by private owners as part of the new development of Greenland. However, it turned out (very quickly) to be the same question of economic capability: the municipalities and the private owners were not able to acquire them, maintain them or restore them, and they were not able to find appropriate uses. This question therefore depends on how society as a whole will be shaped in the future, i.e., how the social, political and economic development is going to take place.

Q. *In the English example, English Heritage is not owner of the property. It helps maintain the property but the National Trust, an organization about 100 years old, is frequently the owner. That situation is a mixture. The National Trust is something like a foundation, and it handles about 1,000 properties (not only monuments but other places as well). Isn't that a good type of solution?*

A. The British National Trust is virtually unique in the world. It owns 500 miles (800 km) of unspoiled coastline. It owns 500,000 acres (200,000 hectares) of countryside and scenic landscape. It owns some 200 great houses, and a number of very important gardens. It has a membership of over 2 million in a relatively small country. It is a phenomenally successful organization that is celebrating its hundredth anniversary, so it is relatively young. (English Heritage is much younger. It owns fewer properties. English Heritage tends to manage ruins such as Celtic properties, Roman ruins and medieval ruins. Its staff jokes about having all the buildings that no longer have a roof on them whereas the British National Trust owns the buildings that have roofs.)

The British National Trust also has a strong philosophy that, whenever possible, the family that originally occupied a great historic house should continue to be associated with the house (in many cases living on an upper floor, living in a wing, living in a portion of the house) so that the properties never become entirely museum properties, but remain (to some extent) family houses. They believe that this keeps life in the properties.

On another front, the British national government has been severely criticized in the last twenty years for sometimes being timid about spending money on major cultural properties. For example, in 1977 a house called Mentmore was threatened. The owner of Mentmore offered to sell it, complete with its contents, for several million pounds. It was a high price, and the British government refused to pay. The owner then proceeded to send the contents of the house to auction, where they brought a great deal more than the price at which the owner had offered to sell. Many people concluded that this was a political mistake by the government.

On the other hand, Calke Abbey was a great house that had been virtually unknown. It was inhabited by an eccentric and reclusive family that never threw anything away. They would fill up a room, close the door, move to the next room and live there. One owner of the house died without leaving a will. His brother inherited with heavy estate tax liabilities. The British National Trust acquired the property, but there was a large governmental infusion to enable the Trust to take the property. It has been an extremely popular property, because things had survived in that house that everyone else had thrown away two generations ago. It took the Trust a long time to do a complete catalogue of all the unusual items that turned up in that house.

In another situation, there was a great house called Kedleston Hall, whose owner wished to set aside substantial sums of cash for his children. There had earlier been an expensive divorce. The house was full of important items of furniture designed by Robert Adam; the owner could have raised large sums of money by selling the furniture. Instead, the house was turned over to the British National Trust, and again a large amount of money was spent, effectively to buy the furniture from the owner, who donated only the house but not the furniture.

In a further situation, there was a house in Yorkshire full of original furniture designed by Robert Adam and Thomas Chippendale, two of England's greatest eighteenth-century architects and cabinet makers. The owner died; there was again a heavy set of estate tax liabilities, and the government made another very large grant so that the furniture in the house could be acquired by the National Trust, which already owned the house.

These arrangements demonstrate, incidentally, that many of the Trust properties are in divided or split ownership; the Trust will own the house and perhaps some parkland surrounding the house, but only portions of the contents. There may be immensely valuable paintings (or silver or other contents of the house) that still belong to the original family, but that are on view in the house. The Trust (when possible) tries to acquire these, so that they will not be sent to auction or sold to museums (or to other owners) and thus be removed from the house.

This shows that even in England, where there is this great scheme called the British National Trust, there are still shortcomings that the Trust is trying to deal with. There are also questions about whether the British government will ever be willing to spend as much money on major properties as it did in the 1980s on the situations I mentioned. For example, much has been said in the past three years about the problems of the so-called "Lloyd's names," i.e., private individuals who have become guarantors for insurance purposes with unlimited liability through the Lloyd's insurance syndicates; many of these people have lost large sums of money, and in some cases their houses have had to be sold and contents sent to auction. This may be a continuing problem. In at least one situation recently, the government simply refused to step in.

ADDENDUM (Katalin Wollák)*

Hungary has tried something similar to the British National Trust. In this transitional period, Hungary established an institution that translates as "Treasury Property Handling Organization." In acquired ownership of some properties that it would like to handle and restore, but after three or four years, it became clear that it did not have the economic or financial resources with which to manage this problem. For the last two years, it has been trying to sell this property and to get private buyers. So the example existed, but the solution was not ready.

---

*Katalin Wollák is an official with the Hungarian National Museum in Budapest.

Administration of Design Controls: New York Case Study

Dorothy Marie Miner*

Subject matter   In formulating an appropriate design review system for alterations to historic structures and landscapes, there are five main questions to be addressed. The following material summarizes those questions, then discusses them in the context of the New York City Landmarks Preservation Commission, which regulates changes to historic buildings. It is not necessarily typical, but provides a useful case study.

Scope   The regulation of design change (and enforcement of the approval process) does not depend on the age of the building, much less whether it is a glorious one-of-a-kind building or only one of the many buildings that make up the identity of a community: each has an importance that society must protect. In regulating design change, the following five questions arise:

1. Who decides whether changes are appropriate?
2. How will change be regulated (i.e., which criteria/procedure)?
3. What property is being protected?
4. What work is regulated?
5. How does the public participate?

1. Who?   The first question is: Who will make decisions addressing proposed alterations to historic properties? Is it an agency, and where would it be placed in relation to other municipal agencies? Would this agency be only advisory and its findings subject to review by other authorities, e.g., by building departments interested in safety issues, and/or by a legislative body?

* Dorothy Marie Miner is a lawyer, planner and past General Counsel of the Landmarks Preservation Commission of New York City. She teaches at Columbia University Graduate School of Architecture, Planning and Preservation, and Pace University School of Law.

In some jurisdictions, the question of whether something is an appropriate change, as found by a historic review commission, may be reversed by a legislative body, e.g., the local legislative body.

2. How?

The next question is: How will change be regulated? This refers to the review of the proposal, i.e., the criteria as to what is appropriate and the procedure to be followed:

Criteria and
Procedure

- Where will those criteria be found?
- Are they listed in the municipal law?
- Is the outcome of the decision-making process the issuance of permits or, instead, of advisory reports?

Nature of
decision

- Is what is issued by the agency binding on the property owner, the local government or the national government? Or is it instead only an advisory report as to what "would be best"?

Compliance

Once an approval has been obtained (whether binding or advisory), the next question is: Does the person comply? Here the issues are monitoring, site visits, violations and legal tools for enforcement, i.e., how do you really know that what the permit authorized is in fact being done, and the steps to take if the work is not in accord with the approval?

Challenges to
enforcement

The small size of staffs of historic agencies creates a problem and makes it hard to make sure that there is compliance with approved work. Finally, in terms of the law, there is the possibility that the agency responsible for noting violations may have to go into court to obtain a court order requiring compliance with its approval.

**3. What
property?**

The third question is: What is being protected from unconsidered change?

Visibility

- Is protection only for the exteriors of buildings or does the agency also have jurisdiction to look at the interiors of buildings when these are significant?
- Is the protection only for what citizens can see from the street or a public space? Or does it include the rear of the building (or an item on the roof), even if no one could see it from a public street or space?

Significance

There might be a different answer given, if an agency were dealing with a landmark or a monument, as opposed to a building in a conservation area (or what, in the United States, is called a historic district). Many of these buildings are not individually of significance, but are included within the boundaries for a historic area.

"Landscape"

In addition to the structures, there is the question of landscape. There is a great deal of interest now in cultural landscapes, e.g., in the little buildings that are part of a farm complex and that (with the way the landscape rolls) represent an important part of the cultural picture in many areas. New York City does not have such large areas, but does have some very famous parks (over 100 years old), designed by Olmsted and Vaux, which are of international significance (e.g., Central Park).

Streetscape

Even in an urban context, a city can have a historic streetscape that it is important to consider preserving: within this streetscape, within a historic area, and in front of landmarks. There may be paving and street furniture (including the lampposts, fire hydrants, even the fire alarm boxes of another age). A 100-year-old cast iron lamppost or firebox gives part of the character to a streetscape.

4. What work?

The fourth issue is what work would be regulated. One may consider a sliding scale of degrees of alteration. In most places, an agency would say that it wants to

Major items

- prevent demolition;
- determine how new construction would fit into a historic area,

Sidewalks and pavement may be part of the character of areas, as in Greenwich Village Historic District. They are of great concern; it is difficult, in some cases, to locate older materials. New York University owns the adjacent buildings (from the 1830s) and is responsible for maintaining the sidewalks. These are "blue stone sidewalks" — large pieces of blue slate that are more expensive to put back than concrete, which the University was hoping to use. The Commission required that the sidewalk remain in the original material. (Joseph Schulder)

or

- determine how an addition to a historic building would work with the existing building.

Lesser items

When an agency reviews applications for alterations, the review often includes lesser items, such as

- shopfronts,
- signs,
- awnings and
- lighting.

Gradual Erosion

But changes to any of these items, though small, can erode the character of what makes an area or a building special: for example, a neon sign placed on a very old building can look extremely inappropriate and can affect its character. An agency needs to look at small alterations that can erode the special historic character.

New York City's agency, for example, looks at proposed alterations of windows. Many people are taking out older windows in order to put in double-glazed windows — windows that

In this building, not only were the awnings installed without the Commission's required approval, but in the area over the main entrance, the owner removed part of the cornice. The owner was issued a "violation," and the Commission made him correct the work and bring the building back into compliance. (Joseph Schulder)

will keep in heat, save energy and keep out noise. These can have a great effect on the outside appearance of a building.

Increasingly, among the challenging alterations are the ones addressed to handicapped access. All over the world societies are much more sensitive to the issue of the need for historic buildings, as well as new buildings, to be accessible, but the result of trying to provide accessibility may mean that there are proposals for ramps for buildings constructed with raised entrances. The question of how to provide access that is sympathetic to the historic character of a building is an issue that will be increasingly important.

Minor work

Review of minor work is also important. This category includes the repointing of the mortar (and making sure that the new mortar has the right colour). Cleaning techniques can be very destructive if done incorrectly. The painting of a building in totally different colors may highlight features in a way that fights the design of the building.

Importance of definitions

So-called "ordinary repairs or maintenance" are often unregulated — either because it is not possible to regulate them or because the decision has been made (as in New York City) that some actions will not be regulated and that people may do ordinary repairs and maintenance without approvals. The question then becomes one of definition: at what point is enough work being done that it rises beyond the level of "ordinary repair" and becomes work that requires approval because it affects the visual integrity of the building?

5. Public participation

The fifth and final issue, in the context of design review and compliance, is the issue of public participation, which in the United States is a very important issue. It can be relevant at many stages in the process; when work is being proposed for a specific structure, there is usually an opportunity to speak at a public hearing or provide written comments.

Generalized support

Private organizations can help to support the work of a design review agency through strong political support. Finally, these organizations can play a valuable role by educating the public about the benefits of historic preservation and the procedures of the agency and by monitoring compliance.

Case study: New York

Those five issues affect the New York City Landmarks Preservation Commission, a city agency.

Multi-level system

One may recall that there are three different levels of government in the United States: the federal level, the state level and the city or municipal level. One of the strengths of preservation in the United States is that it does have preservation laws at all three levels, and they play different roles; no one level could implement a full preservation program. Each complements and supplements the others.

In many jurisdictions it would be useful to have a national or federal program, and a local program. Only on the local level do you get that day-to-day knowledge of historic resources, as well as the day-to-day ability to watch work that is going on under any approval process.

Source of municipal authority

In the United States, there is a great deal of emphasis on local land-use laws, but the authority to have a local law is created by the states: a state authorizes a local community to adopt the law. The local community (the city, town or village) then decides how strong a role it wishes to play in the protection of historic resources.

In the United States, local authorities are the governmental level where a property owner (i.e., a private owner planning to spend only private money to change the building) can actually be subjected to a government decision saying "This is (or is not) an appropriate change."

Regulatory program

In New York City, that decision was made late (in 1965), but the municipal law that was enacted is strong and enables the Landmarks Preservation Commission to deny applications for demolition and inappropriate alterations. If the owner wishes to challenge the City's refusal, he/she must show that as a result, the owner

"Hardship" provisions

- cannot use the building (possibly cannot use it at all), or
- cannot make any reasonable return (i.e., sufficient financial income) from the property. That argument is called a "hardship review." Among New York's 21,000 protected buildings, fewer than ten have been demolished over the course of some thirty years because of hardship.

1. Who decides

The New York City Landmarks Commission is an agency composed of eleven commissioners (some of whom must provide expertise as architects, realtors, historians, planners and landscape architects). There must be at least one commissioner from each of the five major areas of the city, so that there will be a citywide point of view. Although unpaid (except for a full-time chairman), the commissioners are expected to work three to four days per month to carry out the work of the Commission. The people willing to do this are people who care a great deal about the work of the Commission.

Organization

In addition, the Commission is supplemented by a professional staff (which, as of 1994, was about fifty people). There were significant budget cuts in New York City — in 1990, there were eighty people. More cuts are expected, so it is important for this agency to be efficient as it carries out its work.

Activities

The Commission identifies and designates significant historic resources within the city. Once designated, any alteration of a property is subject to review and approval by the Commission. In addition, the Commission has a very small amount of money for grants, and the staff gives free technical advice as it reviews applications for work on the properties.

Limitations

The Commission must sometimes defer to another city agency where issues of safety are involved. The Buildings Department, the Fire Department or the Health Department might say that there is a risk to public safety, and if so, then that agency's order would take precedence over the Commission's decision, and an owner could ignore the requirement to obtain a Commission permit.

2. How regulated

The Landmarks Law is available to property owners in booklet form. The criteria for appropriateness are set out in this publication. For example, the law states that in appraising the effects of alterations in historic districts, the Commission should look at the relationship of nearby buildings and consider, in addition, other factors of aesthetic, historical and architectural value and significance; architectural style; design; arrangement; texture; materials; and

Adoption
of detailed
rules

colour. Obviously, these are broad concepts, which the Commission has interpreted through rules. The Commission has one publication containing its rules, which is also made available to the public.

Reference has been made to the Secretary of the Interior's Standards for alterations. They express widely accepted (even internationally accepted) standards for what is "appropriate" change, e.g., the concept that one tries to keep original materials and disturb the building as little as possible. Such a rule has not been formally adopted by the Commission, but concepts contained in the Secretary's Standards are reflected in many of the rules that have been adopted.

Guidelines

In addition, the Commission has adopted guidelines for some designated areas. For instance, the Commission distributes a brochure for a historic district of nineteenth-century store-loft and warehouse buildings. The guidelines discuss

• the character of a typical store-loft or warehouse,
• what work needs a permit, and
• what kind of work could be found appropriate.

Positive
objective

The brochure also highlights the importance of the granite paving (from the nineteenth century) in this area of the city and the importance of elements like the old loading docks at the front of these buildings. This is the kind of material distributed in order to *help* owners obtain permits quickly for doing *appropriate* work.

Procedure

The permit procedure of the Commission puts the responsibility for assembling information on the applicant. New York City's Commission expects owners to come in with proposed concept plans, but not working drawings.

Application

It has a two-page application form that is very simple, asking for

- the name and address of the applicant,
- the names of the architect and engineer, and
- a brief description of the proposed project.

The real work description is provided on attached documents, which, depending on the scope of a project, could consist of technical specifications, materials samples or architectural drawings. This is what the decision is based on. Even a model could be submitted for a complex proposal.

The Commission has a range of permits depending on the type of work proposed. However, the same application form is used regardless of what permit is requested.

Directions

When the Commission issues a permit, the owner gets a letter describing exactly what has been approved. It will cite the specifications and drawings that have been approved. A set of architectural drawings will be perforated: holes will be put in (with the seal of the Landmarks Commission) to notify the Buildings Department that the plans have the approval of the Landmarks Commission. The Landmarks Commission is the beginning of the process; the Buildings Department is not allowed to approve any permits for a designated building until the Commission has approved the work.

Key: Link to building permit

This treatment of documents is one of the ways that the Commission assures compliance with the law. People who might be casual about historical review are usually not so casual about proceeding without a building permit. This is a key linkage. In addition, a permit card will be issued, which the owner is supposed to post at the building site, so that anyone walking by would know that the work is approved. The permit card will state what the approved work is.

Compliance

Monitoring occurs in several ways to ensure compliance. One way is the staff site visit. A site visit could be focused on some basic issue for a single permit — for example, in the case of repointing, the staff would go to check the colour of the mortar. In the case of cleaning, staff might inspect a sample patch, to be certain that the cleaning will not be too harsh. This is one of the main ways to assure compliance with technical work, as opposed to design work.

Infractions

Following staff visits (to assure compliance with the law and approvals), if the Commission sees that work is not following what was approved (or the owner never came to the Commission to obtain approval in the first place), the Commission has the authority to "issue" (send out)

- a "Notice of Violation" and
- a "Notice to Stop Work."

Court

In order for its notice to have any real effect, the Commission must then go to court. Litigation can be very time-consuming, but on one street there were so many violations the Commission took every owner to court.

On this street the Commission took every single property owner with a violation to court at the same time — all eighteen of them. These two buildings date from around 1820. A gigantic sign, used to cover the upper two floors of the building on the left, had not been approved. In response to the lawsuit, the owners have taken the signs down but must now replace the boarded-up windows with new sashes. In this litigation, the Commission went to court in association with the Buildings Department. Beyond insisting that the owners bring their buildings into compliance with the Commission's regulations, the City sought injunctions and civil penalties against the owners. When there is a violation, the judge can order owners to *do specific things* to correct it under the New York legislation. The owners will have had to pay civil fines for having carried out work without required permits, and the longer an owner takes to bring a building into compliance, the larger the fines. (Joseph Schulder)

3. What property

Dimensions of the mandate in New York

There are now about 21,000 designated buildings in New York City. Most of these are in historic districts. About 1,000 are individual landmarks (i.e., monuments or interior landmarks). Parenthetically, in order to protect interiors, the commission must designate interiors separately, and they must be in areas of buildings that, according to their use, are already publicly accessible. They can be privately owned, but the public must be asked in — to a store, a lobby, a theatre, etc. Under New York City's law, someone's home could never be designated as a protected interior landmark; whether a palace or worker housing, it would not qualify for interior landmark status in the private areas.

4. What work

The Commission staff works to get the quickest appropriate permit issued. There is a choice of three relevant permits:

- a "Certificate of No Effect," often used in connection with interior work, to certify that there is no effect on the exterior; but it could also be used for exterior work, if indeed it was not having an effect on important features;
- a "Permit for Minor Work," issued if there is no building permit involved, e.g., cleaning or repointing;
- finally, the "Certificate of Appropriateness."

The site of this building in Greenwich Village (with the projecting bay window) had been empty, because the house on site in the 1960s was used by Vietnam war protesters to make bombs in the basement, and the whole building exploded and burned. Architect Hugh Hardy acquired the property, but argued that it would be inappropriate to put a replica into that intact row because something important to the 1960s had happened on the site and should be noted. Thus he designed the projecting bay. There were a lot of public hearings, comments and opposition but the Commission approved the design. The lower and upper floors continue the row, so it is a particularly 1970s design. (Joseph Schulder)

In recent years, the Commission has processed approximately 5,000 permit applications annually. Most are either Certificates of No Effect or Permits for Minor Work. Only the Certificate of Appropriateness requires a public hearing: such a project is typically either new construction, an addition, a complex project or a project where the owner's proposal is not found to be appropriate by staff and thus is brought to the full Commission for a decision. Sometimes this work has already been carried out without a permit and the owner wants to "legalize it" *ex post facto* — get the Commission to accept the work that has been done and allow it to remain.

The New York City Commission does not have jurisdiction in a number of subjects where commissions in other cities might have jurisdiction.

This 1840s church in Greenwich Village was a Presbyterian church, but the congregation moved out, and the building was empty. It was bought by someone who converted it to housing. The front of it looks exactly as it did when it was operating as a church, with no windows; but the rest is an illustration of appropriate alterations to make a desirable project work. The Commission approved additions at the rear of the side alleys on both sides, as well as enlargement of windows at the sides of the building, thus allowing light to enter the residential spaces. More importantly, the Commission also obtained *waivers* from the City Planning Commission to allow a less-than-normal size yard and less-than-normal amount of window openings, in order to allow the front of the church to remain unchanged. It is only when one looks down the side alleys that one realizes that the building has been converted to housing. (Joseph Schulder)

Bulk

- New York's commission has no jurisdiction to adopt rules on how large or tall a building can be in a historic district. It can find that a building is "too tall" to fit with its neighbours and deny the permit accordingly but it cannot adopt a rule which specified, for example, that it does not want to see any building more than a certain height. The Commission must decide, case by case, and make individual findings that a particular proposal for a building is too tall to be appropriate for the site.

Use

- Similarly, New York's commission is not authorized to say that a proposed use is inappropriate. When the owner proposes an alteration, the question of keeping an historic use in the building sometimes comes up; but when considering whether the proposed alteration would be appropriate, New York's commission is not authorized to consider the owner's proposed use. Therefore, after alterations have been completed there are many buildings with new uses. In fact, the continuing use of older buildings – where the former use is no longer economically viable, but the new use may be — remains a continuing theme in historic preservation in New York City. For example, old warehouses that can be converted to residential use are very popular and command a high price. They would not command such prices as warehouses.

5. Public participation

The final point is the role of the public in this procedure. Private organizations can play a very important role — for example, in the designation process or design review.

New York has a number of local organizations. There are citywide organizations such as the New York Landmarks Conservancy, which provides property owners with technical assistance and makes loans and grants.

Local support groups

Another such organization is the Historic Districts Council, which helps property owners in historic districts understand the Commission's process. It also monitors work — the Commission sometimes gets calls saying "There's work going on without a permit at such-and-such an address." There are also several groups for specific districts. They show up at public hearings and comment; they help fight for the Commission's budget; they provide education.

Broader support groups

In connection with legislation or in litigation, the Commission receives support not just from the local organizations, but from statewide and national organizations as well, such as the Preservation League of New York State, the National Trust for Historic Preservation and the National Alliance of Preservation Commissions. These statewide and national organizations provide assistance and in times of legislative threats or major court

Conclusion:

cases have helped support the work of the Commission.

New York City's law is an example of a strong law because the Commission can say no to demolition. It is a stronger law than the laws in many other towns and cities in the United States. Even though New York has some of the most valuable real estate in the United States, it has still been able to get a very strong law and keep it in place. In part, that is because of the political support that is coming from these private organizations. The issues New York City's preservationists face are the issues that are faced in all countries, no matter the age of the building and no matter who owns the structure.

These buildings are in the South Street Seaport District. The white building and the one next to it were a case of "demolition by neglect": the owner had left the buildings vacant. The Commission had approved work in the 1980s, but the owner never did it. The buildings became unsafe, and the Buildings Department issued notices to "seal or demolish." There were court proceedings and ultimately, when the owner failed to act, the City obtained a court order authorizing it to demolish. The Commission succeeded in having that order amended, and the City was allowed to stabilize the buildings instead. Parenthetically, the only practical reason the City was able to carry out the work was because a gift was received from a not-for-profit organization that financed the additional cost of stabilization over demolition. Demolition would have cost $100,000; stabilization cost $225,000. (Joseph Schulder)

Participants' Questions

Q. *I am concerned about gaps among building components. Let us suppose that there is a particular building where part of the cornice had been removed. What happens to those materials that have been removed and how do you replace them?*

A. First, the Commission does not usually know what happens to those materials because by the time the staff gets to the site (or the neighbours call up) they are gone. In the case of blue stone sidewalks, for instance, the stones may be so smashed that they cannot be reused.

When an item had to fit into a narrow area, such as between the remaining portions of an original cornice, the Commission approved using a different material for that portion of cornice. If the missing element is metal, the Commission may require metal as the replacement, but terracotta pieces are much more of a problem to fit back in. The Commission definitely allows alternative materials.

Q. *The Commission deals primarily with facades. Could you be more specific about its jurisdiction over interiors?*

A. It has jurisdiction over interiors in only two ways. One, the Commission would have jurisdiction to the extent that interior work affects the exterior, e.g., the owner put a wall or stair up against a window so that it could be seen from the outside and would interfere with the facade. The Commission can say no to that.

In addition, it can designate esthetically and historically significant areas of the interior that are publicly accessible. It has designated restaurants, and many Broadway theatres have designated interiors. It has designated office lobbies — the Chrysler Building and the Empire State Building have designated interiors.

It cannot designate an interior that is private, i.e., one to which the public is never invited. Although there are seventeenth-century houses in New York, it cannot designate and protect the interiors of those houses and make sure their features remain.

Q. *Concerning the urban development aspect of your work, let us suppose that there is a historic district that exists as an ensemble. If the owner wants to build a new structure in this district on the site of a demolished structure, does your agency have any influence on the character of the facade of the new building?*

A. Yes, it reviews and approves the design of all new construction in historic districts. There are several examples of residential rows where a building came down before the historic district was created; when the owner wants to build a new building, the Commission has to approve the design. The same principle applied to the building that had blown up in the 1960s in what is now a historic district. The Commission had to approve the new design. Any work that goes on within the boundaries of a historic district — even if the building is not that significant — comes under Commission review because even a building that is "not-contributing" can be made less compatible.

Q. *If the Commission does not give permission because it believes the new building is not appropriate or does not harmonize with the surrounding context, is the Commission's decision final and definitive?*

A. If the Commission found that a proposed new building was not appropriate, it could say that it did not fit and deny the permit, so the owners would not get to build it subject to the hardship provisions.

Q. *Does this approach apply to any existing element that was not appropriate to the historic district?*

A. The Commission, when it creates a district, must take the conditions as they exist at the time of designation, so if an existing building does not contribute to the character of the district, it is allowed to remain, and any previous changes that are not appropriate are allowed to remain. On the other hand, any new construction after the vote to designate must be appropriate. It is reviewed as to its relationship to the historic buildings found around it, its massing, materials and colour, texture, scale, etc.

The Commission will try to make sure that a non-contributing building continues to play at least as harmonious a role as possible. In many cases, this may mean that a later building (for example, a 1930s building among buildings dating from the nineteenth century) is true to itself. The Commission will not try to make its signage look like nineteenth-century signage (it would merely try to make it "fit" the store fronts and designs for a building of that period). In short, the Commission must approve any new construction in the district and any additions — even on empty lots and non-contributing buildings.

Accessories: The Diverse Case of Fittings and Furnishing in European Legislation

*Peter Rupp**

International pressures

The interiors of historic buildings have been affected by events in Central Europe, namely the opening of frontiers and the creation of a new market of antiques. These interiors, as well as independent movable objects, are exposed to important financial pressures, as they are elsewhere in the world. Indeed, the intervention of organized crime in this area makes it increasingly difficult to protect objects of artistic and historical value, and most of all to preserve them *in situ.*

Incidental protection

Cultural properties, protected by law as historic monuments, are still gravely threatened; cultural properties without any legal protection are in even greater danger. That is why it is important to analyze implicit protection opportunities for cultural objects not affected by direct — explicit — measures. These opportunities may derive eventually from the protection of the buildings for which these objects are "accessories." The following is a brief outline of solutions that have been adopted by several European systems.

Accessories defined

This outline covers a variety of things that resemble one another only in that

- they fall somewhere between buildings and movables, and
- they are protected implicitly with the building of which they form part.

The exact line drawn between such objects, on the one hand, and buildings or movables, on the other, depends on the definitions used in national law. It would be incorrect to define

* Peter Rupp is a graduate in law (Vienna) and economic history (Paris). He is the Senior Research Officer of the Department of International Affairs of the French Ministry of Culture; he also heads the European Directory of Heritage Policies for the Council of Europe.

them universally as *"immeubles par destination"* (as the French call them), i.e., as objects intended to be immovable, since some countries do not include the owner's intention among their definition or criteria. The English expression "fixtures and fittings" is larger, but the term "accessories" corresponds even better to the general concept.

The key is to determine whether these accessories are implicitly protected by the law governing the building of which they form part, since the possibility of preserving them *in situ* depends on such implicit protection — unless they are protected in their own right. The following are thus the main questions that we will consider in connection with the countries covered.

Key questions

1. Are accessories that form part of buildings covered by national legislation concerning cultural heritage? If so, are they precisely defined? What criteria are used to distinguish them from movables?
2. Are these accessories implicitly protected as monuments with the building of which they are part?
3. What happens if the accessory is removed from the building? Does it retain or lose its protected status?

Italian version

In Italy, the Act of 1939 on the protection of property of historic and artistic interests protects both accessories (*"pertinenze"*) and the buildings of which they are part.

Inconsistency

The Italian Civil Code, to which the specific heritage legislation refers, defines *pertinenze* as items of property intended for the permanent service and embellishment of another item of property and states that legal transactions and relationships applying to the principal item apply also to the *pertinenze*. Regardless of the wording of the Act, however, *pertinenze* are interpreted in Italy as being objects materially attached to the building, and the criterion of intended use does not come into play. This has the following consequences:

- accessories are protected with the building of which they form part, only if they are firmly attached to it physically;
- if they are, the effects of protection continue even when they are removed from their setting;
- on the other hand, objects that can be removed without damage to themselves or their buildings count as movables and require separate protection in law. In Italian law, for instance, the famous Baptistry Doors in Florence are "movables."

Initiative

The protection of buildings as monuments is implemented by the relevant supervisory authority, i.e., the external service of the Ministry of Cultural and Landscape Assets, at the regional level. Protection is ordered by a ministerial decree that is served on the person concerned (the *notificazione*) and entered on the supervisory authority's regional schedule of registered properties. There is only one level of protection.

Spanish
counterpart

In Spain, the Act of June 1985 on the historic heritage of Spain defines a range of items that may be declared of cultural interest:

- For buildings, there is only one level of protection and this is conferred by royal decree (issued on the proposal of the Minister of Culture or the autonomous community concerned).
- For movables, there are two levels of protection. Such items may be declared to be of cultural interest (the stricter level), but also may be registered in the general inventory of movables forming part of Spain's historic heritage (a less strict level of protection).

In Spanish law, the following two categories of items are covered when buildings are declared of cultural interest:

Definitions

(1) All objects located in buildings declared of cultural interest and considered immovable in the Spanish Civil Code; this includes (a) anything attached to the building, or (b) placed in it by the owner in a fashion showing that it is *intended* to form a permanent part of the property, and (c) all machines and apparatus intended by the owner for use in connection with work conducted on the property and required for that work.
(2) All objects that may be considered inseparable from the building because they form or have formed part of the building or the building's *decoration*.

Removal

These objects are still protected if they are removed from the building, even when they constitute independent units and can be used for other purposes and even if the removal does not seem to detract from the building's historic or artistic value.

Alternative
declarations

The Act also recognizes the cultural interest of all movables located in a building that has itself been declared of cultural interest, provided that such movables are identified in the declaration as being an essential part of the history of that building.

Notwithstanding this implicit extension of the declaration of cultural interest, the items it covers are very often protected by a separate declaration, either collectively through a general reference to their presence in the building concerned or individually.

Belgian
counterpart

The Belgian Civil Code, like the French Civil Code, makes a distinction between objects immovable by nature (*immeuble par nature*) and objects immovable by intention (*immeuble par destination*). The protection of buildings covers movables

- that form part of them, or
- that have become immovables by intention.

This approach is confirmed by the Decree of 1976 regulating the protection of monuments in the Flemish region. In the Walloon region, the Decree of 1987 copies this provision. The Order of March 4, 1993, regulates matters similarly, in the Brussels region, including, in the concept of a building, fittings, pictures or decorative elements that form an integral part of the structure.

Contrast

Unlike the French system, Belgian legislation on the protection of monuments follows ordinary law. Objects immovable by intention (and implicitly protected as monuments with their buildings) retain their protected status when removed from the building of which they form part. In France, on the other hand, these objects when removed from the buildings again become movables and lose their protection under the specific heritage protection legislation.

Initiative

The items of property are classified as monuments in Flanders, Wallonia and in Brussels by royal decision (given on the basis of opinions prepared for the Royal Commission on Monuments and Sites by the specialized heritage department of the governments of Flanders, Wallonia and the Brussels region).

Dutch counterpart

The Netherlands' legislation on historic buildings is confined to immovables. Movables are protected by a separate act, the Cultural Heritage Preservation Act.

The Monuments and Historic Buildings Act lists the elements that may be protected by law. Included are all buildings that are at least fifty years old and of public interest by reason of their beauty, scientific significance or cultural and historic value. Accessories are not included in the Monuments and Historic Buildings Act. Accessories forming part of buildings are implicitly protected by ordinary Dutch law.

The new Dutch Civil Code distinguishes between immovables, movables and components and further divides components into things that are components because

- they are used as such, or
- they are physically attached to something else.

Under this new civil code, all components (attached or not) are covered by the laws applying to the main object. This means that components retain their protected status even when separated from the main object.

British counterpart

The four parts of the United Kingdom (England, Wales, Scotland, Northern Ireland) sometimes — but not always — have different laws (e.g., a law may apply only in England and

Scotland) and are administered by different public authorities (e.g., one ministry is responsible only for England, another only for Scotland, for historical reasons).

There are always separate laws on the various areas of cultural heritage. Strictly for the purpose of this report, I will refer to England (which forms 54 percent of the surface area of the United Kingdom and has 83 percent of its population) and Wales (which covers 9 percent of the surface area of the United Kingdom and includes 5 percent of its population).

Categories

England and Wales protect

- archaeological sites, through the Ancient Monuments and Archaeological Areas Act of 1979 (as amended);
- buildings, by the Planning, Listed Building and Conservation Areas Act of 1990; and
- movables by the Import, Export and Custom Powers Act of 1939.

Initiative

Protection of a building starts when it is listed as a historic building by the official of the Commission, established under the Ministry of National Heritage, named English Heritage, the government body responsible for protecting historic buildings. Listed buildings are graded in one of three categories depending on their historic and/or aesthetic importance.

Reform

Until 1990, fittings and fixtures (accessories) could not be implicitly protected by listing of the building to which they belonged, since the authorities wishing to protect them were required (at the time that the building was listed) to indicate the exact scope of protection by furnishing a detailed inventory of the elements covered. The new planning act of 1990, however, breaks new ground by treating the following as part of the building (and protected as such):

- all objects or structures attached to the building; and
- all objects or structures within the building's area (within the curtilage), which although not attached to the building, have formed part of the property since at least July 1, 1948.

Application

The Act does not, however, indicate what kinds of objects are covered in practice by the categories it uses. The following are generally regarded by the protection authorities as accessories within the meaning of the act: stairs, panelling, balustrades, window and door frames, fireplaces, balconies, glass and tile, etc.

As well as the physical criterion of attachment, the criteria of legal ownership and of artistic and historical value are now applied.

Removal

These accessories may be removed only with the permission of the local authority concerned with Listed Building Consent, and the legal effects of protection continue to apply to any object removed without this consent.

German counterpart

In Germany, the federal system has the following consequences: the protection of movable cultural assets (along with regional planning, nature conservation and construction) is the responsiblity of the federal government; the protection of buildings as monuments is constitutionally a matter for the sixteen *Länder* (federated states), which all have specific legislation and administrative structures for this purpose.

In the *Länder*, monument protection is implemented by the cultural affairs minister (the title varies), who has legal authority to take all the relevant statutory decisions and is assisted by the specialized conservation service (*Ländesamt für Denkmalpflege*) whose activities precede decision making and include

* inventorying monuments,
* maintaining and restoring state monuments,
* providing advice and financial assistance for private owners,
* working to heighten public awareness, and
* in general keeping the list of monuments.

Protection starts when the building to be protected is entered on the list of monuments. There is only one level of protection in Germany. Accessories are covered in the various federated laws on the protection of monuments.

As in many other areas of law, the formal legislative independence of the *Länder* does not prevent the sixteen systems from displaying considerable homogeneity in practice. The following applies to Bavaria, which is illustrative but not necessarily identical to all other *Länder*. The 1973 Bavarian act on the protection and conservation of monuments (as amended) makes a distinction between

(1) "historic accessories" intended for the architectural monuments in which they are found (*historische Ausstellungsstücke*) and
(2) "movable monuments" (*bewegliche Denkmäler*).

Implicit protection

The "historic accessories" are implicitly protected with the buildings concerned and do not need to be entered on the list of monuments in order to benefit. The Act puts castle gardens, for instance, in this category, along with frescos, murals, altars, communion rails and church bells, which are normally included. These items have a different status in France, for instance.

Procedural
distinction
To enjoy legal protection, movable monuments (i.e., those not specifically intended for the buildings in which they are located) must be entered on the list of monuments. Once entered, they are protected. Listing is very restrictive, applying only to movable monuments of capital importance. At the end of 1990, 88 movable monuments had been listed in Bavaria, as against 110,000 buildings.

Contrast
The criterion used to distinguish historic accessories from movable monuments is above all historical.

Criteria
The essence of a historic accessory is its unified, coherent connection with an architectural monument. In principle, physical attachment is not a criterion, even though most historic accessories are firmly attached to the buildings of which they form part. Historic accessories may be planned as part of the building from the outset (*ursprünglich geplant*) or added to it later (*hinzugewachsen*). They do not necessarily match the building interior in style but must date from a specific completed period (*abgeschlossene Periode*) in the past and must not be reconstructions.

In practice, many implicitly protected historic accessories are entered on the list of monuments as well, as a precaution.

**Austrian
counterpart**
Austria is also a federal state, although the constitution places monument protection under federal jurisdiction (in Germany it is under *Länder* jurisdiction). That distinction is based on history: Austrian federative elements have always been provinces, well integrated in the Habsburg territory; German *Länder*, on the other hand, are successors to the ancient German states of the nineteenth century which were subjects of international law. These are radical differences.

In Austria, the 1923 Act for the Protection of Monuments (*Denkmalschutzgesetz*, as amended) regards monuments as all man-made immovable or movable objects whose preservation is in the public interest by reason of their artistic, historic or cultural importance.

The federal monument conservation service (*Bundesdenkmalamt*), which is answerable to the minister of science and research, decides whether preservation is "in the public interest" in specific cases. There are two main scenarios:

Automatic
protection for
"public"
property
- In the case of privately owned monuments, these must be expressly designated as being of public interest in order to be protected.
- In the case of public or quasi-public property (i.e., owned by the State, regional or local authorities or other public law

bodies, foundations, hospitals or state-recognized religious communities), the law assumes that the requisite public interest automatically exists unless the federal office decides to the contrary.

Criteria

The federal office always applies the same criteria to public and private property in deciding whether protection is in the public interest. The historic, artistic or cultural importance (on which the law bases its definition of "monument") may be intrinsic in the objects themselves, but may alternatively derive from their relationship to other objects.

Groups/ collections

The provisions applying to individual monuments thus apply, too, to groups of buildings and collections of movable objects if these groups and collections form a unified whole by reason of the historic, artistic or cultural connection that exists between them, including their location, and if their conservation as a whole is in the public interest because of this connection. Regardless of the other possibilities logically inherent in the wording of these phrases of this act, the official interpretation applies these provisions only to architectural complexes and collections of works of art.

Procedure

To qualify as monuments, accessories forming part of a building (whether attached or not) must be the subject of an explicit decision by the federal office.

Alternatives

The Austrian system provides for a simultaneous protection of a building and its accessories within a single procedure when three conditions are satisfied at the same time:

(1) The accessories in question must be firmly attached to the building;
(2) they must be shown to be historically part of the building; and
(3) the accessories must be mentioned individually in the protection document.

Moreover, the declarations of protection made under the laws of the Third Reich have never been reviewed and are therefore still in force. According to these declarations, simultaneous protection of buildings and their accessories was accomplished by a collective mention of the accessories. In order for this form of implicit protection to be valid, the accessories must be firmly attached to the building.

Results of overview

This admittedly brief survey of specific legislation on monuments shows that accessories forming part of buildings are covered by literally all specific heritage protection laws except in the Netherlands.

Extent

The definitions distinguishing accessories forming part of buildings from movables are based on:

Criteria

- historic and artistic criteria (in Bavaria and probably in all German *Länder*, and in the United Kingdom);
- historic, artistic and material criteria in Belgium and Spain; and
- material criteria only in Italy.

Effects
on removal

These definitions, which provide the basis for legal protection of accessories as historic monuments, determine whether the effects of protection continue when the objects in question are separated from the buildings of which they form part (as it is in Bavaria, Belgium, Spain, Italy and the United Kingdom). Unless otherwise provided by specific heritage legislation (as in the Netherlands), the state of accessories is determined by ordinary law.

In the law of some countries, the general rule providing for implicit protection of accessories (under the instrument that protects buildings) is more in the nature of a declaration of principle. In the absence of detailed and binding definitions, this not only leaves the door open for separate protective measures for each of the elements to be protected but positively calls for them.

In other countries, the legislation allows a global protection that covers accessories by identifying them as "an essential part" of the building, as it is in Spain, without listing them separately in the protection document. In some countries, the "implicit protection" is believed to be a more modern and progressive form of protection, but in practice it is nowhere really efficient. So, even in states that have precise definitions in their legislation, accessories implicitly protected by law are often simultaneously covered by separate, individual and explicit protection clauses as a precaution. From a legal standpoint, these must be seen as declaratory measures that confer no extra status.

PARTICIPANTS' QUESTIONS

Q. *Monuments do not exist simply as architectural objects but also within an environmental context. The land around the structure or object may also be of great significance. Indeed, various restoration efforts can actually damage the cultural layer or stratum (e.g., the archaeology) and thus affect the cultural value of the monument or structure. In the legislation that you analyzed, how does preservation relate to the environmental envelope and landscape, as well as the archaeological issue?*

A. It is true that in all European countries, we have to work to harmonize law and administration; perhaps the ideal goal should be to obtain unified protection systems for all aspects of architectural and natural heritage and environment at the same time.

ADDENDUM (Lisbeth Saaby)

It was a surprise to hear that the famous Ghiberti doors in Florence are considered as movable objects. I would have thought they were just part of the building, i.e., part of the immovable object. Of course they can be taken away, just as the windows can. I would have liked to consider them as part of the immovable building.

In Denmark, the preservation of buildings law can protect the immovable building with its fixtures (e.g., with its fireplaces, door frames, tapestries, etc.) but the protection cannot cover the movable objects (e.g., the chairs, porcelains, paintings, etc.). However, there is one provision in the Danish law that provides a financial framework for arrangements with the owner to preserve valuable objects *in situ*. It provides this possibility only when the movable objects form an architectural and/or historical part of the total unity with the building.

This provision has existed since the law came into force in 1980; it has never been used (although several attempts have been made), but it was inspired in reaction to one actual case, where the beautiful contents of a valuable and famous castle were in danger of being split off. The agency and the owner negotiated an arrangement in which a foundation (a trust) was set up, supported financially by the State and the regional authority. This trust acquired all the movable objects in the castle, so the private owner still owns the land and house (and can dispose of it, of course, within limits, which derive from the listing of the building), but the trust owns all the movable objects. This arrangement has existed since 1978 and has functioned very well.

A country has to balance the interest of the private owner, who still has the use (to a certain extent) of the building, the chairs, the porcelain, and so on, with the interests of the State and the public authorities and the public, which now also has access to the building and the interior.

This was a pragmatic solution, perhaps very Danish.

ADDENDUM (Peter Rupp)

I am informed that the Danish buildings preservation law can protect not only the building, but also the fixtures belonging to the building; it cannot protect, however, the movable objects. It also provides for special arrangements with private owners (in order to preserve valuable entities of objects *in situ*), although this provision is rarely used. The protection of a building under the Danish law thus does not automatically include the whole of the interior of the building, fixtures and fittings. Indeed, the completely implicit protection of interiors, as under the building legislation, does not appear to exist elsewhere in Europe.

Concerning the doors of the Baptistry of Florence, their juridical status results from the Italian Civil Code to which the specific heritage protection law refers. The code provides its definitions of accessories: since the doors can actually be removed, they are deemed movables.

ADDENDUM (Stephen Dennis)

There was a dispute (which now seems ended) between the J. Paul Getty Museum in California and the English government over whether the Antonio Canova statue of the Three Graces could leave England. In the background was an earlier dispute between English Heritage and the Dukes of Bedford, over whether the statue had become in fact a "fixture." When it had been commissioned in the early nineteenth century by a Duke of Bedford, a special structure called the Tempietto (or "little temple") was built at Woburn Abbey to house the statue. English Heritage argued in court that the statue had become a fixture and was therefore legally attached to the Tempietto and hence was covered by the listing of the immovable. The Duke of Bedford argued that because the statue had been included in the inventory of various personal trusts that had been set up in that country, and the acceptance of the contents (movables) of those trusts by the English government for tax purposes, the English government could not therefore argue that it was a fixture (part of the immovable) and personal property (movable) at the same time.

The decision in that earlier dispute, therefore, was that it could be sold. It was sold, and the dispute with the Getty Museum over whether it could leave England then followed.

I think this is an example of how ambiguous some of this legislation can be, even in countries that believe they have anticipated all options that might arise.

Q. *When looking at developments within the European Union, what are the prospects for assuring that the movable cultural object will not leave the country? Although every country has its own protection for movable objects, the European Union will open the borders.*

A. The opening of the borders, the "single market" (i.e., total liberty or circulation of persons, goods and capital within the European Union), has no effect on the *immovable* cultural heritage of the different Member States. Whatever the European actions of programs may be in the field of immovable heritage (exchanges, use of new technologies, professional training, etc.), all these actions are carried out on the basis of selective decisions of the Member States. The states remain entirely responsible for immovable heritage. In this repect, the European Union did not make legislation.

It is not the same for *movables*. Movable cultural objects are directly affected by the single market. The new situation required introduction of special legal provisions, because

- on the one hand, the cultural heritage (and therefore cultural objects, especially those defined as "national treasures" that cannot leave the territory of their state), remains entirely within the competence of the Member States, according to the *Treaty of Rome* of 1957 (Art. 36);
- on the other hand, the single market that excludes systematic border controls within the Union makes the control of the circulation of cultural objects very difficult.

In order to ensure the protection of the cultural heritage of the different Member States, the Union has therefore adopted two legal texts:

- the "Regulation" of December 1992, which provides protection along the external borders of the Union, by subjecting the export of cultural objects to third countries to an authorization issued by the state where the object is situated. (A European "Regulation" is applied directly as is, within the Member States.);
- the "Directive" of March 1993, which represents a system of restitution of "national treasures" that had left (illictly) the territory of a Member State. (A European "Directive" is not applied as is, but its normative content is transposed into the different national legal systems, in a way determined by each state.)

An annex, relative to both texts, specifies the categories of cultural objects concerned (with respect to age and financial criteria).

In France, the implementation of the Directive has been carried out in the form of

- a law (December 1992), and
- a law enacted to enforce this law (January 1993).

According to this legislation, every movable cultural object affected by the European Union legislation has to be covered by a Certificate issued by the Ministry of Culture, attesting that the object in question is not a national treasure and is therefore free to circulate within the Union or to be exported to third countries.

Part IV:

Inducements for the Private Sector

The Economics of Physical Planning and Land-use Regulation

Myron Dornic*

Regulation and economic backdrop

The effectiveness of physical planning and land-use regulation issues related to conservation may involve a number of dynamic forces at play in a market environment:

- Regulations may attempt to deal with economic forces to create development incentives that are conducive to or compatible with conservation goals.
- Other regulations are designed to directly regulate elements of a development scenario.

"Pareto optimality"

Regulation inherently involves a change in the allocation of rights. In framing considerations dealing with land-use allocations, an overriding concept should be one of "Pareto optimality."§ Pareto optimality means a focus on those changes in allocation that are capable of making everyone better off.

For example, competitive markets are intended to produce allocations that enhance Pareto optimality. Placing land in private ownership is intended to produce efficient exchanges so that Pareto optimality can be obtained. It was thought that expansive grants of property rights would accomplish this most quickly. In the United States, for example, historic emphasis on such grants is credited with the rapid development of land resources.

"Externalities"

It must be understood, however, that there are forces that may interfere with the efficient operation of market forces. A service or disservice among agents for which there is no channel of mediation (i.e., no means of market response) is termed an

---

* Myron Dornic has degrees in law, land-use planning and special education. He specializes in land-use law at the Dallas law firm of Jenkins & Gilchrist.
§ Named for Vilfredo Pareto (1848-1923), whose Treatise of General Sociology (1916) has had an important influence on all the social sciences.

"externality." The land market has many externalities.

- For example, the activity on one parcel alters the value of other parcels;
- the restoration of a building's beautiful historic façade may be appreciated by the passerby — and may enhance the value of a neighbouring property;
- restoration of an entire district may be the "highest and best use" of historic resources and may ultimately produce the most value for the greatest number of persons.

Cost vs. benefit for the individual

However, if there is no mechanism for the passerby or the neighbouring owner to contribute to the restoration, the building owner may underinvest (i.e., invest too little) in the cost of the restoration. This is because the cost of the restoration may be more than the single property owner is able to recoup *personally*. Under those circumstances, the owner will tend not to invest the amount that produces the greatest good.

Example

For example, a pre-conference tour showed a restoration in progress, where the building owner had intended to install a large picture window rather than to restore the Gothic windows that would have been correct for the building's original façade. The problem of the externality arises in exactly this case. The individual property owner, who may benefit from being in the historic district and from the enhanced value that has accrued to all the properties there due to restoration activities, nonetheless expects to derive the most individual value if he/she is able to have a restaurant, for example, containing a very large picture window with an expansive view towards the charming district.

In that example, the competitive market alone will not produce the Pareto optimal results for that individual interested owner. It is also obvious that if everyone is given licence to install picture windows, the goal of optimal enhancement will not be realized by any of the owners in the district or by the public at large.

Further examples

Moreover, even if we are able to get beyond the problem of the individual interested owner, we have further problems:

- Individual owners may not always be rational actors.
- Individual owners may not always have the resources with which to produce the Pareto optimal result.

Implications for intervention

Therefore, from the standpoint of strict economic analysis, both regulation and incentives remain appropriate for dealing with externalities in the land market to produce Pareto optimal results with regard to conservation.

Scenery

Another example is the protection of a scenic countryside. Protecting scenic beauty may produce a benefit that enhances the value of an entire region. However, aside from government expropriation, there is virtually no method whereby all of those who benefit by the beauty that has been preserved can contribute to the individual property owner who must bear the financial brunt of keeping the land in a relatively undeveloped state. Again, because of such externalities, it is appropriate to create a "pseudo market" — to intervene in the private market by means of such devices as fees, taxes, subsidies or direct government regulation.

Direct
regulation and
the paradox
of success

One problem that arises in the competitive market is that increases in population (or simply the popularity of a restored district) result in pressure to provide newer and larger development to accommodate the interests of those who wish to reside or work in such a district.

If no regulation or other devices are used to control the market, individual property owners will have an incentive to raze smaller historic structures in order to realize the benefits of increased rents from larger, more modern structures. In countries like the United States, this has been a problem because the

Controlling
the "envelope"

land-use regulations have usually been intentionally designed to promote development. Most cities have regulations that allow for huge "envelopes" (i.e., allowable outer limits) of development. As demand for property increases, the incentives for realizing increased rents put great pressure on historic resources. One way of removing some of this economic pressure is to provide regulations for new development that will limit new development to historic patterns; regulations for new development can be designed so that the new development may not achieve an increase in building mass or density. Such regulations can include

- limiting height for new development,
- limiting density,
- enforcing traditional setbacks from property lines,
- limiting mass, and
- enforcing historic street patterns.

Related
regulations

In Paris, for example, the Rue de Rivoli has retained its character by historic regulations that mandate a uniform cornice line and set limits on heights. In other cities, regulations are also being developed to accommodate the automobile in manners that will not be destructive to historic patterns. New developments should not be permitted to have façades taken up with garage entrances, and buildings should be required to have entrances at pedestrian levels. In addition to removing some of the economic pressure for replacement of older structures, such regulations promote new construction that preserves the scale and character of a place and reduces the likelihood that new construction will damage historic views.

Regulatory
incentives

Conversely, it may be appropriate in some cases to grant density bonuses, i.e., to allow increased use or development in areas where such use or development will not damage the historic resources. In the United States, this is sometimes done with the "transfer of development rights."

TDR

A transfer of development rights (TDR) system sets up a market for development rights that can be transferred from one property to another. It operates as follows:

- First, it presumes that a private owner is restricted from using property to its fullest development potential because of conservation goals.
- The owner is allowed a credit for the development that has been forgone. These rights are formalized into "development units."
- The owner is then allowed to use those rights/units on other property to develop that "receiving property" to a greater intensity, e.g., to a greater height or to produce more floor area than would otherwise be allowed.
- To provide some fluidity in the market, the owner of the protected resource need not also be the owner of the receiving property: indeed, the owner is allowed to sell the development units to owners of property in a receiving area.

Necessary
conditions

This is a somewhat complicated system to maintain, and will work only if

- there is development demand in the receiving area; and
- in the absence of TDR, the regulations in the receiving areas would allow development only at a level that is somewhat less than what would otherwise be acceptable; if, on the contrary, the receiving areas have extensive development rights to begin with, there will be no market to purchase any more rights (to develop to a greater degree). If this were the case, the owner of the conservation property would have received nothing in value for forgoing more intensive development.

Preferential
uses

Another manner in which owners of historic resources can receive compensation for engaging in conservation activities is to provide a system of bonuses that a property owner can use on site. Some cities, for example, have allowed higher-rent uses to go into areas usually reserved for other uses, if the higher rent uses are being housed in historic structures. For example, in Dallas, Texas, there are Victorian houses near the downtown, in what has traditionally been a residential area. The City of Dallas has designed its typical regulations to continue to encourage residential uses in and around downtown, but there is also a demand for office space in this part of town. To encourage retention and conservation of historic homes in this area, the City has allowed certain smaller office uses to be contained in the residential district. Office uses are permitted, however, only if they are housed in historic structures. Because the office uses can get higher rents than residential uses, many structures are being conserved rather than being replaced with newer residential buildings.

Zoning

The policy of cities in the United States has been traditionally to plan for a mixture of uses permitted in various geographic areas within its cities. Cities would set forth a listing of all the uses that would be permitted in a typical "zone" of the city. All listed uses would be allowed, and the market would then determine the ultimate resulting mix of uses. However, some American cities, (e.g., San Francisco) have designed programs to limit the uses that will be allowed within an area designated for conservation. The City of San Francisco had seen a trend developing. Very large stores wanted to go into older retail areas — areas with accumulations of older buildings with small store fronts. In many cases, historic resources were lost because promoters of large retail stores were tearing down buildings that would not accommodate large retail uses. To restrain this trend, the City of San Francisco has outlined districts where there are now limits on the number of large users that will be permitted in the district. Therefore, buildings are being saved, even where there is a demand for large-scale retail uses.

Use quotas

Development quotas

San Francisco also puts a numerical limit on the amount of new office space that can be constructed in highrise structures per year. The effect has been twofold:

- First, there are limits on the number of structures that are lost to accommodate new development.
- Second, the regulations strengthen the market for renovation. Because new construction is cumbersome, there is increased pressure to renovate rather than tear down older structures to accommodate the demand.

Compromises

Other forms of incentives include a relaxing of standards for historic resources. For example, most cities in the United States require that the owner or tenant of a building provide parking nearby to accommodate people who will be visiting the building and using automobiles. This requirement is usually expressed in terms of a certain number of parking spaces in a ratio to the amount of floor space contained in the building. Because Americans have a love affair with the automobile, and because they despise traffic, these parking requirements tend to be strict and expensive for property owners to comply with. Many cities, however, have realized that historic buildings were seldom designed to accommodate automobile uses. To provide an incentive for a property owner to conserve an historic building, an exemption is often adopted to relieve the owners of historic buildings from the requirement to provide off-street parking spaces.

Such accommodation (e.g., of building codes and development standards) can be applied to other topics as well.

Tax incentives

The major source of revenue for most American cities is to tax property owners on the assessed value of the real estate that the owner holds within the city. Each building (and the land on which it rests) is taxed, based on the value. To provide tax incentives for property owners to conserve historic buildings, historic buildings will often be assessed at a lower rate for tax purposes. Alternatively, a city may exempt historic buildings from taxation for a certain number of years following the building's renovation or restoration.

Another method of using fees or taxes for conservation purposes is to provide a tax on services or goods and designate a certain amount of such tax to go to conservation purposes. In Texas, for example, cities have some control over how to spend taxes that the state imposes on the rental of hotel rooms and on sales taxes collected on restaurant meals. Such revenues amount

Tourist tax

to a tourist tax. Hotel rooms can be taxed at a percentage of the cost of the rental, or a flat fee can be charged for each hotel room rented. Because there is often a direct link between the conservation of historic resources and tourist dollars, many cities are choosing to use revenues collected from hotel and restaurant taxes to fund conservation purposes.

In an interesting twist on this idea, fundraisers in the city of Hartford, Connecticut, have come up with the idea of a "viewing tax." To help pay for the restoration of Hartford's Old Statehouse, proponents of the conservation project have asked for donations from businesses located in nearby buildings from which one can view the Old Statehouse. Proponents of the conservation effort have suggested that such corporations pay a viewing tax. Suggested levels of contribution were based on the number of windows that the corporation or business had facing the Old Statehouse. Because the laws in Connecticut do not allow the imposition of an actual tax on the viewing of a conservation property, this effort is not a real tax but a totally voluntary contribution. It shows, however, how creative some cities and private organizations have been in raising revenues for conservation. It may give ideas for voluntary or mandatory programs elsewhere.

Summary

These are just some basic ideas regarding what various cities have done to promote conservation purposes within a private market. They suggest why interventions into the private market can be appropriate to achieve these purposes. These ideas may assist those who will be developing tools for conservation in countries that are moving to a private-property free-market system.

Participants' Questions

Q. *What are the specific uses that the City of San Francisco has set quotas on? What is their justification to limit those types of uses?*

A. The quotas are often tied to a commercial use of a specific floor size. For example, in a commercial area with small shops, the City may feel that it is appropriate to allow one to three larger clothing stores in the area (this will provide enough flexibility to promote a strong concentration of shopping uses); but the City may legally declare that there will be no more than three clothing stores larger than 5,000 square feet (500m²) or may declare that there will be no more than seven restaurants greater than 8,000 square feet (800m²) in the area.

The justification is this: the City was seeing large commercial users coming in and eliminating the former character of the area by taking advantage of the people who were there and offering a large "cafeteria"-type use. This was not particularly appropriate, and it created market pressure to raze smaller buildings to make way for larger floor plans.

Q. *How does Texas protect its capital (Austin)? Is there a local ordinance (i.e., edict) that protects the views of the Texas state Capitol building? How effective is the ordinance? How popular is it?*

A. The approach taken in Austin is based on "viewsheds" (i.e., sightlines or vistas). There are approximately a dozen viewsheds defined in the Austin ordinance, in a radial pattern around the Capitol building. No construction may obstruct these sightlines. Certain decisions were made about which avenues have the most significant views, and views from those or from points of interest were the ones most protected. As far as its continuing popularity is concerned, there was originally a wealth of public support for this idea. I suspect that it retains much of its original popularity, although it is a very complicated ordinance for the city to administer. It requires technical skill for the people who are permitting construction to know exactly where these angles fall on a particular property.

ADDENDUM (Stephen Dennis)

Those of us who have forgotten everything we once knew about trigonometry would find it a very confusing ordinance, because it is defined in terms of trigonometric functions to determine how high a building on a specific location can be before it interferes with one of the protected sightlines.

ADDENDUM (Myron Dornic)

To some degree, the complications in that ordinance prompted developers and even city staff to apply pressure for changes, because it is so complicated to understand.

Q. *How is the planning process dealing with the automobile? How does the automobile fit into sustainability issues?*

A. We are seeing changes in the way that planning deals with the automobile. There is some discouragement in the manner in which the automobile has been accommodated in the United States. To a large degree, people believe that if you build a highway, it will fill up — and if you build it larger, then that would just encourage more people to use the automobile instead of transportation that would be more economical or resource-efficient. Many feel that the United States spent a significant amount of money on improving highways, and there seems to be no corresponding benefit in the reduction of traffic congestion.

Consequently, and because the automobile produces such detrimental effects on air quality, there has been significant pressure placed on planners to plan for other methods of transportation. These have always been a part of the planning scheme, but the preference in the United States has favoured highways because of a perceived public preference for travelling individually in automobiles.

The planning process is now looking at ways to encourage people to at least share automobile rides; special transit lanes are being put in place to bypass intersections and are reserved for buses or people who are travelling three or four to a car.

The United States still has a long way to go in changing its planning policies, to give as much emphasis to mass transit as it does to the automobile. There is also a stronger move now in the United States to develop more areas where people can work, live and have leisure activities all within walking distance.

ADDENDUM (Marc Denhez)

The international declarations tend to be negative on the subject of the automobile, but seldom specify how communities should deal with this problem. In the case of historic districts, a number of paradoxes have been discovered.

One paradox was that according to conventional wisdom, one of the typical reasons why historic districts were having so much difficulty (e.g., commercial areas), was because they were "so difficult to get to," it was "so difficult to park," etc. Therefore, the main question was how to provide parking, and the typical answer was to oblige the renovators of buildings to provide a certain number of parking spaces. What did that do? It simply discouraged restoration.

Another mistake was to assume that such problems could be solved by simply improving the ability of traffic to move through the historic district. This was considered "terribly important": communities, for example, would ban parking so that the traffic could move in more lanes, and they would make all the streets one-way streets so that traffic could move even faster. However, the faster that traffic moved, the faster these communities realized that people were driving through the historic centres so that they could go to stores at the very periphery of the city to park and and shop *there*. By the time that planners had finished reorganizing all the traffic in the historic centre, the result was to cause a crash in economic activity in the centre. The automobile is not as easy to deal with as some may assume, and it is not safe to rely on mere intuition.

Q. *On the subject of environmental regulation, is it better to have federal legislation or local legislation?*

A. There may not be any "right" answer to that question. In the United States, local governments are often competing with one another to draw new industries to a particular area. To some extent, the drafting of environmental regulation (such as regulation on air emissions from the automobile or from industrial sources) is probably best accomplished at the national or federal level, because local governments might prefer incentives to attract industries that produce emissions (so that they can provide jobs to local people and be taxed).

On the other hand, states and local governments have tended to be much better at enforcement because they know their particular area. For example, the regulation of floodplains and wetlands (or areas that are left as habitats for marsh birds, or to provide extra flood capacity) have been fairly well administered on a more local level in the United States. There may be some federal legislation that is in place, but it may be administered locally.

Q. *What kinds of penalties should be put in place for property owners who do not behave in the way that they are required to by law? Should there be a system of monetary fines or something else?*

A. There are different penalties in different localities in the United States. The City of Miami Beach has a number of art deco buildings that are considered very good examples of architecture from the 1950s and earlier (1930s and 1940s), but properties were being destroyed for new hotels. The City had a system of penalties, but it was to the property owner's benefit to demolish the building — and pay the penalty — rather than to act in accordance with the regulations.

One of the most effective means, although somewhat difficult to administer, is to insist that if a property owner illegally destroys a historic building, the owner will be required to rebuild it. Of course, owners can never truly recreate what they have destroyed; but, on the other hand, this obligation removes the incentive for them to realize the greater profit. The laws in the United States will allow the government, if a property owner refuses, to do the reconstruction in the property owner's place and charge the property owner for that reconstruction.

Sometimes the issue is merely a change to a certain element on a building. For example, the property owner may be changing a sign and may be refusing to put back the historic sign (or refusing to take down a sign that is not in keeping with the regulations). The laws in the United States may allow the local government to remove the sign on its own; the property owner is usually required to receive a notice that the government intends to do this if the owner does not behave in a timely fashion. The legislation may require the local government to go to a judge to ask permission, i.e., an order to go ahead with the correction that is needed. Then the owner can be charged for the cost of that correction. If the owner not want to pay, a lien (a charge or civil law privilege) can be assessed against the property, so that it is just like a mortgage for the purchase of the property; if the property owner wants to sell, the land records will show that there is a lien on the property, and any proceeds from the sale of the property must first repay the government for the lien. In a worst-case scenario, the government can actually foreclose on the lien and sell the property. The government will retrieve the costs that are owed to it for the restoration, and the remainder of what is left in value will be returned to the owner (because it was the owner's property).

Tools in Attracting Private Investment

*Susan Mead**

* Susan Mead is a partner in the 650-lawyer firm of Jenkins & Gilchrist, Dallas. She has over fifteen years' experience in land-use law.

Background

The objective of professionals such as myself is the organization of neighbourhood groups to form consensus-based planning efforts, between neighbourhood groups and the private sector (e.g., developers) in the construction of new buildings, the revitalization of old buildings and the construction of new neighbourhoods

Dallas
case study

There are economic development incentive tools in the United States; we have "packaged" them in Dallas, and the city is currently attempting to use them in the downtown to restore the major buildings that are left. That package of tools has been "exported" to Fort Worth, Houston and San Antonio. These financial tools can be used anywhere in the United States; they may not be applicable to places like Central Europe yet, but they could be at some point, particularly as the tax system evolves there.

Initiative

Partnership

The financial tools that Texas is experimenting with stem from legislation that was put on the books many years ago — but is not particularly geared to historic preservation. Anyone who intends to use it should limit its use to the revitalization of historic buildings. If those measures are combined with private actions, the result is a partnership between the government and the private citizen — but usually the initiative comes from the private sector. It is not usually government-imposed: it is the other way around.

Specific
taxes for
improvements

The first tool is a "public improvement district." A public improvement district introduces an additional tax used in a specific geographic area for specific public improvements, such as special lighting, landscaping or public parking areas. Because of the additional tax, this approach is not an "incentive." It could even be a disincentive — so the legislation could be specifically written to exclude a landmark building or monument from having to pay the special assessment.

Examples
of activities
covered

For example, in one public improvement district in Dallas, the purpose was primarily to fund a trolley (a tram). In the 1950s, the city had torn up its trolley tracks and now the district is putting them back — at substantial cost. New street lights are also being funded in the historic district, as well as extra security (there are mounted horseback patrols, which the district pays for: that is not typical security; it is additional security).

The district has special banners and festivals, which the district pays for through this public improvement district tax: each property owner pays an additional tax to fund these improvements. For example, I own a building in the historic district, and I pay an extra $100 per year. In this particular case, the district produces approximately $500,000 per year for these improvements, for ten years.

Procedure

The public improvement district is established by deciding what the community wants to use it for. First, the concept is described in an informational package addresssed to the area. Its boundaries are determined. Then a petition is circulated to every property owner in the proposed district. Over 50 percent of them have to agree that they will pay the special tax by signing the petition. Finally, the petition is presented to the city council and the council passes an ordinance (a municipal decree) to create the district.

The typical information sheet is very simple, showing the schedule for the creation of the district and for the improvements that are expected to occur.

Earmarking
new tax
revenue

The second financial tool is a "tax-increment financing district." Unlike the previous example, taxpayers continue to pay the same tax that they would pay anyway. It is not an additional tax, but the difference is that the increment, i.e., the increase in property taxes that will occur (because buildings have been restored, or new businesses or offices have moved in), is deposited into a special fund, reserved for the special district.

This is exceptional because in the United States, when property tax bills are paid, the money usually goes entirely into a general revenue account for the city, and the city distributes the money city-wide via a vote in a budget. Tax-increment financing is virtually the only vehicle that lets taxpayers redistribute the tax dollars without a vote of the general populace.

Examples

This tool has been used all over the United States, primarily in California. The City of San Diego has thirteen tax-increment financing districts; Miami has two. There are about twenty of them in Texas now. Dallas has five; the first one is in an area called State-Thomas.

Specific
example

The State-Thomas area had approximately 100 residents in a 65-acre area (± 25 hectares), 15 acres of which was historic (6 hectares). The residents joined in planning their area, (for about four years), and what resulted was a new land-use plan and a public improvement district. In order to fund the public improvements (such as street lights, water, sewers — things needed to restore and build new buildings), owners and residents did the planning, turned the results over to the city, and now are in the process of implementing the plan. In a city like Dallas, it was a challenge to deal with the juxtaposition of building sizes. The district also had ±40 acres (±16 hectares) of open space. That was not a result of a bombing — although it looked like it. One property owner had gone in with a bulldozer and cleared it; there are many depressed areas in Dallas where this occurred in the 1980s. This owner/developer has now left all of this raw land in the middle of the city. (I restored fifteen buildings in the district, primarily because Dallas was losing so many buildings. Three of us decided to buy as many buildings as we could, and then we resold them.)

Zones were created within the area, namely an interior neighbourhood district, an office district on the freeway edge, a housing zone and a small but intact historic district. Almost 3,000 units were created on and adjacent to the vacant land in less than four years.

Who pays for
services?

The purpose of the tax-increment financing district is to allow someone who wants to restore a building (or someone who wants to build a new building) not to have to pay for water, sewer, landscaping, lighting, etc. (i.e., any of those services that a city would normally provide), which cities are now reluctant to provide (because they no longer receive the level of federal funding in our country that they were used to). Cities today will typically look to the private sector, and the private sector's response is to start using these kinds of tools.

Refunding
permit fees
and other fees

The other tools that Dallas is using as part of the general focus of preservation of the few remaining larger historic buildings left there include fee rebates. When an applicant files plans for a project, the applicant normally pays a building permit fee to the City, but if the building is an historic building, the applicant gets the fee back. Similarly, if there are water or sewer hookup fees, the applicant gets them waived or refunded.

Code
advice

If the project has building code problems, a specialist is assigned to work through the code issues as they relate to a historic building, because the code may not actually work for that building because of its age or location on a site.

Loans for part of project

The newest program is called "gap financing." In order to convert some of the older office buildings — built in the late 1800s or early 1900s — into housing, which is needed and useful, there is a gap between

- what makes sense economically
- and what the project will actually cost (usually it is a substantial gap of several million dollars).

Dallas now has $25 million to spend in one area in downtown Dallas to provide gap financing for developers who want to convert these historic buildings, i.e., if their bank loan and equity (private capital) still fall short (e.g., by two or three million dollars) for the project, there is a special fund they can go to to borrow the needed money at a low interest rate.

Property tax freeze

The next form of economic development tool is tax abatement, which is tax relief. Taxes are frozen at the pre-redevelopment level. If an owner wanted to install central heat, new electricity and new plumbing, theoretically the value of that building would go up and theoretically the tax bill would go up. Dallas freezes taxes at the pre-renovation level for a period of up to ten years.

Tax exemption

Dallas also has the ability (and is now using it), to grant 100 percent tax exemption to a historic building. In the case of several downtown buildings, the effort to save them means that the owner pays no taxes for up to ten years.

Business programs

Another method called an "enterprise zone" designation is not often utilized, but it could be. It applies to areas that could be considered pockets of poverty; it is meant for distressed areas, to attract new businesses and create jobs. It has little direct relationship to historic preservation — although it could, if tied directly to historically designated landmarks. Owners of businesses located in these zones are eligible for sales tax rebates as well as fee rebates (including rebates on municipal taxes).

Special municipal borrowing

"Certificates of obligation" are perhaps more problematic, because cities in Central Europe, for example, have probably not yet acquired the authority to issue bonds, which is a typical method of borrowing private money. U.S. cities borrow masses of money through the sale of municipal bonds. A certificate of obligation is typically a small bond — say, $4 million — that is sold so that a public project can be funded quickly without competitive bidding and without going to the voters for a vote to allow the city to borrow the money. These bonds are extremely useful to do a quick project when a building is threatened, e.g., when the conservationists need the money and the city wants to acquire the building.

Fees

"Entertainment-use fees" represent a method that probably looks familiar. A charge is made for admission to a museum, and the money is put towards the maintenance of the museum. That is not a new idea. In Texas, however, there is talk about doing what several other states in the United State have already done, i.e., enacting an entertainment-user fee that would place a tax on tickets to sporting events (like football games and basketball games) and that would put the money from that tax into a special fund for cultural events for non-profit organizations. This could be an extremely lucrative source of funding for cultural activities.

Reduction of income tax

Finally, the State of Texas has not created historic landmark tax credits. However, many American states have historic landmark tax credits, modelled on 1980 federal legislation (that was virtually eliminated in 1986). A developer could get a credit against income tax for the certified rehabilitation expenditures on a historic building. There were criteria, e.g., the rehabilitation expenditures had to be incurred within twenty-four months; the costs had to be substantial for the buildings to qualify; and the rehabilitation had to be approved by the state historic commission both before and after reconstruction.

Case study

Fort Worth, Texas, is an interesting final case study in how to guide the private sector. There are two individuals in Fort Worth who own thirty-nine square blocks of the downtown. Fort Worth will be different from any other American city because these two have the control and the money to do a first-class job. They will be using a tax increment financing district. The purpose of that district is to build an underground parking garage with a park on top to help serve the new performing arts hall; to put in place a public market area; to update an underground subway system that feeds in from a fringe parking lot into the centre of downtown; and to add street trees and lights.

It is expected that the project will produce an increase in sales tax revenue (there is an 8 percent sales tax in Texas) because of the increase in development that these private parties have promised to put into place. The tax dollars that will go back to the different taxing jurisdictions such as the school authority, the junior college authority, the hospital and the county authorities. Over a twenty-year span, we should have generated thirty to forty million tax dollars to spend just in this district on public improvements. And it should be a remarkable project.

147

Participants' Questions

Q. *Who takes the initiative in launching these measures?*

A. The economic development tools at the federal and state levels were enacted by our Congress and our state legislators.

The initiative and choice to use them usually come from the private sector. A group from the private sector reads the law, puts together a plan and goes to a city or a state legislative body and presents what it needs and then gets it done. It is private-sector initiated, although most of the laws were already on the public-service books. These laws may need to be amended, but not often.

Q. *Is your model of neighbourhood organization for extra services workable only in rich neighbourhoods or in other neighbourhoods also?*

A. The State-Thomas neighbourhood (the first one I referred to) had 100 residents. There were probably twenty-five yuppies (young urban professionals) and about seventy-five were members of minorities and not very prosperous. We worked together, successfully.

Q. *Do you have a single level of taxation for these special fiscal measures, or do you differentiate for people of different economic means?*

A. There are two answers. First, some of our laws allow people over sixty-five years of age to stop paying property taxes or to pay at a reduced rate on their homes; so if the owner is over sixty-five, the problem can easily be handled. Second, if they are not over sixty-five and the taxes are a burden, and if they live in one particular area, it is possible to treat that particular area differently in the original petition.

If they are spread out all over the district and they are not over sixty-five, there is a problem. So far, my clients have not had that problem. We have either had people over sixty-five, or we have established a tax reasonable enough that they haven't minded paying it for the extra services. It's a give-and-take.

Q. *What do you say to critics who object that such measures are so demanding that they are not feasible except in big American cities?*

A. Those arguments — opposing historic tax credits and other modifications for historic buildings — are among some of the same arguments I heard within the United States in 1979 and 1980, when we passed our most successful legislation for preservation, i.e., the tax credit act. "Too complicated!" "We need the money!" Don't believe it.

ADDENDUM (Stephen Dennis)

It took a national tax policy conference (sponsored by the National Trust for Historic Preservation and held in 1976, with about 500 people attending), to push the federal tax incentive legislation forward. The Trust then published the conference papers as a book called *Tax Incentives for Historic Preservation*, which was reviewed on the front page of the *Wall Street Journal* and became a kind of bestseller for about three years. It is possible, with the right luck and circumstances, for tax policy issues to become a matter of wide public discussion.

ADDENDUM (Susan Mead)

Some countries would like to know what the private sector can propose constructively to the government, instead of the government telling the private sector what to do. If countries write good legislation so that the private sector can use it (e.g., a proper tax credit act), then they can do far more for the rehabilitation of historic buildings than by dumping a large amount of money on a city and saying, "Go spread it out."

The tax credit act in the United States was the one thing in the last ninety years all Americans can be extremely proud of, because it did work.

Part V:

The Voluntary/
Non-profit Sector

Fundraising, Membership and Non-profit Organizations

J. *Myrick Howard**

Role

In many countries, including the United States, non-profit organizations (i.e., non-governmental organizations) are an important component of historic preservation efforts, whether at the national, state or local level. Often, governmental agencies (the public sector) are most involved in identifying and evaluating the historic and architectural resources, while non-profit organizations are often key players in implementing protective strategies, sometimes as advocates (urging a favourable response from the public or private sectors), sometimes as direct participants.

The following represents the U.S. situation, which has counterparts in many other countries.

Ownership

A non-profit organization has certain unique characteristics.

- It is not owned by any individuals or corporations. If it ever goes out of business, its holdings are transferred to a similar non-profit organization, never to private individuals or corporations.
- Its assets and income are to be used only for the benefit of the public.
- Its records are available for public inspection.
- The organization pays no taxes, but must report on its finances annually to federal and state authorities.

Administration

A non-profit organization is governed by a board of directors that is elected according to procedures spelled out through bylaws (i.e., organizational rules) that have been approved by the Internal Revenue Service, which is the tax-collecting authority of the U.S. government. Usually, the board members are

---

* J. Myrick Howard has degrees in city planning and in law (U.N.C.). Since 1978, he has been the Executive Director of Preservation North Carolina.

nominated by a committee of the board, and often they are elected by the organization's membership. Membership is generally achieved by the payment of dues.

Role of donors

Most non-profit preservation organizations are set up so that contributions are deductible from the income taxes of the donor. When a donor gives money (or other items of value, such as stocks or real estate) to the organization, he/she pays less tax to the federal and state governments.

Typical funding strategy

Most successful non-profit preservation organizations have many donors of modest amounts as well as a few donors of very large gifts. Funding will come primarily from individuals, with other sources being foundations, businesses and governmental agencies (often for specific projects). Organizations seek to find dependable sources of funds, such as endowments (investment money set aside for the production of income) or forms of earned income (such as income from tourists or royalties from the sale of books).

Role of board

A major responsibility of the board of directors is ensuring the financial health and well-being of the organization. The board establishes and monitors the budget, and it bears the legal responsibility for raising sufficient funds to carry out the budget.

Typical nomination strategy

Some directors may have been asked to serve on the board because of their ability to make substantial financial contributions. Others are elected because of their contacts and their reputation in the community. Still others are included because of their knowledge about the historic resources and about preservation.

A frequently heard saying about board membership is "Work, wealth and wisdom — any two will do."

Volunteerism and staff

Most boards do not pay their directors, even for expenses. In fact, many boards require directors to make a financial donation to the organization in addition to their contributions of time and talents. Therefore, directors of a non-profit historic preservation organization must have considerable interest in historic preservation and commitment to the organization. Most non-profit organizations begin as purely voluntary enterprises, adding paid staff only after achieving a level of security.

The addition of staff greatly increases the cost of operation, but it adds continuity and professionalism. It becomes someone's paying job to oversee the well-being of the organization. The roles of the board and volunteers are not reduced by the introduction of staffs; the staff reports to the board of directors and must work closely with volunteers. The transition from a volunteer organization to a staffed organization can be very difficult.

Mandate

The work undertaken by a non-profit preservation organization can vary widely: advocacy, public education, technical assistance, property stewardship, and real estate intervention, to name a few. Above and beyond the preservation work (undertaken by the organization), fundraising is necessary for doing the work.

Extending influence

Advocacy usually takes the form of lobbying legislative bodies for the adoption of policies, laws, and funding favourable to historic preservation. Lobbying may include drafting bills to be considered, cultivating legislative leadership, rallying public support and thanking legislative supporters afterwards. Non-profit organizations often serve as legislative "watchdogs," making sure that laws unfriendly to historic preservation are not adopted.

Education

Public education takes many forms. For one thing, there are many different preservation constituencies to consider:

- Building owners need information about how to properly renovate and maintain their properties.
- Contractors and labourers need to be taught respectful rehabilitation.
- Local government officials need training about the implementation of preservation regulations.
- Preservation professionals need continuing education.
- School children — and their teachers — need instruction in order to ensure that future generations share an interest in preservation.
- And the general public must be reached, through promotion of visitation at historic sites, publications, media contact, and so forth.

Seldom can a non-profit preservation organization do all forms of education well, so usually it must set — and periodically re-evaluate — educational priorities.

Expertise

Non-profit preservation organizations offer many different types of technical assistance, ranging from providing detailed architectural plans for building restoration and maintenance to simply serving as a clearinghouse for telephone inquiries. Often an organization will rely on a network of volunteers to provide technical assistance.

Museum property

The acquisition, ownership and operation of historic properties open to the public is often the initial impetus for the creation of non-profit preservation organizations. Many non-profit organizations have begun from a small core group of persons interested in preserving a particular endangered historic landmark. The building often ends up open to the public as a museum, attracting tourists, school children and local citizens. Though expensive to maintain and operate, these museum properties serve an important role as many persons' first introduction to historic preservation. Numerous volunteers and professionals in historic preservation were initiated into preservation through involvement with a museum property.

Property
transactions

More sophisticated non-profit preservation organizations actively enter into the real estate market for the purpose of preserving endangered historic properties. Such an organization might

- acquire an endangered historic property,
- market it to potential purchasers, and
- sell it with protective "covenants" (i.e., servitudes that obligate the purchaser and future owners to renovate and maintain the property).

By direct intervention in the real estate market, the organization can help assure the preservation of troubled properties. The covenants then protect the property in the future. Such intervention is referred to as a "revolving fund" (so-called because the funds obtained from selling Property A are used to buy Property B, then upon sale of Property B, those funds are used again for Property C, etc.).

Example of
revolving fund

The non-profit organization with which I work, Preservation North Carolina, has developed a national reputation for its revolving fund work. Since "revolving" (buying and selling) its first property in 1977, the organization has found sympathetic purchasers for more than 200 properties. More than $50 million has been invested in those properties.

Many of the properties with which the revolving fund has worked have been in very deteriorated condition and in rural areas. In many cases, the most difficult job for the revolving fund is getting owners to agree to part with properties that they have owned for years, and to let someone else purchase and restore them.

Market impact

The revolving fund advertises these properties through a variety of media and co-ordinates inspections by thousands of potential purchasers. More than 4,000 people call Preservation North Carolina each year to inquire about properties for sale.

Conditions

Once the properties are sold, the purchasers are responsible for restoration and maintenance according to agreed-upon standards. With each property, protective covenants are placed in the deed transferring the property to new owners.

Goal

Creating a successful non-profit preservation organization is not easy. Many publications have been produced about how to create and operate non-profit organizations successfully. One of the most useful functions of a non-profit preservation organization is building a network of interested preservation activists, who gain strength through their association.

Non-profit preservation organizations work best when they work closely with public agencies and officials, private individuals and businesses, and other non-profit organizations. Co-operation and collaboration build strength for the preservation movement. Non-profit organizations can be a vital ingredient for building a vibrant preservation movement in a community.

Frequently, older buildings are in such poor physical shape that almost no one recognizes their aesthetic potential to the community. Indeed, countless important buildings are lost that way. In North Carolina, Preservation North Carolina was nonetheless successful in organizing the rehabilitation of various significant buildings which, prior to the beginning of the project, would have appeared improbable even to ardent conservationists. In the case of the Lentz Hotel (top), the Sanderlin-Prichard House (middle), and the Parrish House (bottom), their potential was underestimated — until this voluntary non-governmental organization did the work above. (J. Myrick Howard)

Part VI:

Case Studies of Transition

Legislative Strengths and Hurdles in Slovakia

Katarína Kosová*

The Institute

The protection of cultural monuments in Slovakia has a long tradition. It follows the Central European tradition, and it recognizes the well-known art-historical schools of thought of this region.

Our Institute for Monuments was created in the 1950s and began work in a systematic manner to map the cultural heritage in Slovakia.

Individually targeted property

Thanks to this work, we now have registered 13,000 immovable cultural monuments and approximately 15,000 movable cultural monuments. I say that we have "approximately" 15,000 movable monuments, because the Institute is currently working to *re-document* the sacred monuments in this category for basic identification purposes and to survey their current physical condition from a conservation viewpoint. This work is also being done because of the increasing theft of our movable monuments and because they were insufficiently documented from the beginning.

This comprehensive program of documentation will certainly identify several thousand additional movable monuments, and the most valuable of these will be added to the central list of monuments.

Groups of property

The Slovak cultural heritage is protected not only through the listing of individual items, but also through the identification of larger groups. Slovakia has seventeen "Town Monument Reserves" and ten "Reservations of Folk Architecture," and it is now working on a program to identify and list smaller areas

---

* Katarína Kosová, Ph.D., heads the Slovak Institute for Monuments in Bratislava.

called "Monument Zones." There are seventy of these, and work is continuing to identify more.

The most important individual objects are identified as National Cultural Monuments, and there are now seventy of these as well.

Administrative framework

The following is how the Slovak collection of nationally recognized cultural properties is classified for administrative purposes. The governmental administrative structure for the preservation of monuments in Slovakia is centralized in the Institute (which is a part of the Ministry of Culture). The head office is the Institute for Monuments, which has its main office in Bratislava. There are eleven regions, each of which is administered through a regional centre. Regions are further sub-divided into local offices, which exist where there are clusters of cultural resources to oversee. There is a total of twenty-five offices (i.e., including both regional and local offices) outside of Bratislava.

The Institute has 160 professional specialists on its staff. It is recognized as an expert organization and provides binding advice to various governmental administrative offices (the County Offices on the county level and the District Offices on the local level). It works very closely with these governmental offices.

Enabling legislation

The current Slovak law took effect in 1987. It does not adequately cover the needs for monument care in the current situation, not only because the system changed, but because of a host of complex problems, notably that the system contains loopholes.

Pre-existing situation

The original law talked about "ownership rights and responsibilities" and set forth "the function of the State in monument care." At the time when that law went into effect, the State already had a monopoly on ownership of the monuments and often on the restoration of the monuments. That arrangement was a lot "easier" to administer because it was essentially the State talking to the State.

Massive transition

Current difficulties on the general legislative front are further complicated by the fact that a new or better system of dividing our country into counties and/or regions is likely to be developed.

Uncertainties of devolution

A further problem is that the delegation and decentralization of national responsibilities to local or county governments has not been completed — nor is it yet completely clear how this may finally evolve. Therefore, legislative problems are not solely a matter of how far our privatization activities have moved forward: it is necessary to weigh all of the above factors in preparing the new law.

Acceptance of international duties

With the break-up of Czechoslovakia, many national responsibilities (which had been centralized in Prague) needed to be assumed by the new Slovak government. The Slovak government had to start making its own relationships on the international level, rather than letting all arrangements be made through Prague. This included ratification of the World Heritage Convention by the Slovak government and the creation of a Slovak ICOMOS Committee.

Integrated legislative process

The Ministry of Culture has been working carefully for four years on new legislation. At the same time as the law is being prepared, the system is becoming clearer (as the Slovak government's responsibilities are more fully recognized and ratified). Once all of these problems have been resolved on the general government level, the preparation and ratification of specific historic preservation legislation will be easier.

Problem solving

The Institute prepared several variations of the law, including an explanation of the basic problems that new historic preservation legislation should resolve:

- some of the problems are purely procedural,
- some are questions of financing, and
- some address the ultimate administrative organization of national responsibilities.

Funding

The funding for monument restoration in Slovakia includes three governmental players:

- the State fund for conservation, called ProSlovakia, which partially funds selected projects for restoration of cultural monuments;
- the Ministry of Culture, which is also the owner of many cultural monuments that are used for public purposes, and which therefore invests significant sums from its own budget for their restoration;
- the Ministry of the Interior, which has county and district offices where private owners of monuments can ask for grants for restoration. (Unfortunately, the sums that the Ministry of the Interior has to offer in this fashion are not very high.)

Financial proposals

Two years ago ProSlovakia had 120 million Slovak crowns to spend on monuments — and this year it had approximately 20 million Slovak crowns. That is a very significant difference. Conservationists have therefore proposed several methods for financing monument restoration through non-State involvement.

163

It is not expected that in the near future, Slovakia will reach a situation where the State can simply eliminate all the existing state-funded programs for monument restoration. Alternatively, the drafters of the new legislation have considered not only the national budget, but also the budgets of the municipalities as sources of funds.

However, new methods have been proposed, because the evolving new Slovak economic system is being built on the assumption that private individuals and businesses will have increasing funds to invest (and the national government may therefore plan to turn its direct attention and resources to other matters). In response, we may need to consider the following:

- new sponsors and foundations;
- low-interest governmental loans;
- some form of tax incentives.

Facilitation

Furthermore, because the Institute can already require owners of historic properties to meet certain research criteria and carry out work to certain standards that the Institute both sets and enforces, there is a question whether it might be advantageous for new legislation to permit the Institute to provide free historic research (and perhaps other services to owners without charge) as an additional incentive to monument restoration.

Hazards

This period is very serious for monument preservation. With all the problems facing conservation, even the proposed laws (to date) do not sufficiently solve the problems and therefore need additional review. We seem to be in a blind circle: our work gets to be a matter of faith, i.e., that "in time" our society will have a "different outlook" on the whole question of monument care. It is a difficult task, but it is hoped that with the support that should be provided by the proposed new law, conservation will succeed.

From a professional viewpoint, the Institute trusts that the proposed new law will not trigger a return to the starting point, i.e., a total re-evaluation of why historic monuments are important and which should be protected. We trust that the efforts to date have indeed been professional and have provided strengths on which to build, rather than problems to solve and strategies to replace.

Public acceptance

The current Slovak legislation creates a certain positive framework for the care of monuments — and conservationists accept that legal situation, as do those who actually enforce the preservation law and those who are the owners. It is surprising that in North America strict sanctions for harming a cultural monument are possible, while the sanctions under Slovak laws are laughably mild in comparison. For many people here, it would be more profitable to damage a monument than to follow the law.

The economic thread

In the world that Central Europe lived in for so many years, the financial aspects were not always brought to the forefront. Instead, the mindset insisted that it was "uncultured" to talk constantly about money and the costs of restoration. It is now important to understand that what is called commercial can create a situation where people can become prosperous, and through this prosperity, goals can be reached.

The challenge: "selling" preservation

The key to understanding the serious economic problems faced by conservationists in Central Europe is to consider the question of historic preservation as an idea to "sell." Even I find myself somewhat slow to accept this concept — in light of the fact that I was immersed in an organization whose "business" was already historic preservation. But it will be up to us to be more accepting of this concept, and to take it on as our own.

Legal, Administrative and Financial Measures in Hungary

*András Petravich**

Modest
numbers

Hungary has only a modest number of historic monuments, as a result of its stormy history. It has 10,200 protected buildings, 25 conservation areas, some 1,000 legally protected environments and fewer than 200 movements designated by specific decision. Altogether, these ensure legal protection for less than 1 percent of the building stock of the country.

Paradox

The international reputation of monument protection in Hungary is due instead to the high professional standard of a few outstanding restoration projects, and to the active Hungarian contribution to the work of international organizations on monuments and cultural heritage.

Nevertheless, simultaneous with these achievements, the general state of Hungary's monument stock has been getting worse since World War II.

Legislative
background

The institutional protection of monuments in Hungary dates back to the mid-nineteenth century. Hungary's first historic preservation act, passed in 1881, was very up-to-date for its time. In 1949 this act was replaced by a law-decree, and since then, Hungary has had no preservation act *per se*. Since 1957, the mandate for protecting monuments belonged (at any given time) to the Minister responsible for construction. Its fundamental rules were included, in 1964, in the Building Act and its executive decree. A departmental order of the Minister for Construction contains the rules concerning the protection of monuments in detail. These three laws are still in force, with several amendments, the most important of which are those of 1991 and 1992.

* Dr. András Petravich, M.A. Arch., M.Sc. C.Eng., Dr.techn. Arch.Conservation, Hon. Chief Counsellor, Senior Research Worker, Hungarian Museum of Architecture, National Board for the Protection of Historic Monuments.

Movables and
immovables

The legislation deals with immovable monuments and so-called movable monuments (i.e., museum relics) separately. The latter are dealt with in the laws for museums, as well as for archaeological sites.

Current
management

According to the above-mentioned laws, monument protection is today controlled by the Minister for Environment Protection and Regional Development. For cultural policy concerning monuments, this Minister acts in concert with the Minister for Culture and Education.

The National Board for the Protection of Historic Monuments (OMvH) [succeeding, in 1992, the former National Inspectorate of Historic Monuments (OMF) founded in 1957] works as a government agency under the Minister's supervision and is responsible for the departmental and official control of these activities, and for the research and documentation activities concerning monuments. As a preservation authority, it supervises all kinds of work in connection with monuments in the whole country. In the case of protected buildings, it acts as a building authority, too; but in the other cases, it acts through the local building authorities.

The Board has two institutes:

- the State Centre for Restoration of Monuments (ÁMRK), organized from the sections of the former Inspectorate in 1992, and
- the Institute for the State Care of Monuments (MÁG), established at the same time, with a mandate for which there was no institution before.

The Board now has a staff of 250; the two institutes together have 150 employees. The organization and duties of the Board have been determined by a special departmental order.

Categories/
Procedure for
protection

For the moment, Hungary has three categories to protect single buildings, and two categories to protect zones. The two responsible ministers together are entitled to register monuments in the form of a departmental order, issued on the basis of a proposal made by the Board.

Legal effects

Monuments can be used only in accordance with their character, and their historic and artistic significance. The use can be altered only with a permit from the Board. The Board can oblige the owner to admit the public. The Board has to supervise the state and use of monuments continuously. Monuments have to be maintained by the owners, at their own cost. The Board can oblige the owner to carry out the necessary work on the monument or can have it carried out at the owner's cost. For any intervention affecting the physical state, use or artistic value of a monument (as well as the legal status of a State-owned monument), a permit or consent from the Board has to be obtained. By departmental order, it is possible to expropriate properties for monument protection. The State has also the right of first refusal in certain cases. Finally, departmental orders determine some special procedures.

Construction
standards

There are some eighty other laws with rules concerning monuments. For example, the Construction Code orders the protection of existing objects and details of architectural value and provides exceptions from certain construction requirements for construction work in existing buildings. It also allows authorities to depart from security and similar requirements in individual cases — if these cannot be met according to the Code, but there is an *equivalent* solution.

Current
transition

In these years of transition, the laws affecting the former State-owned properties are very important. The objective of monument protection is present in these laws to varying degrees, but less in the field of privatization, where the economic approach is prevailing.

Economic
context

After temporary successes in the mid-eighties, the financial rules now have no regard, once again, for the interests of monument protection. Monuments are now exempt from only one tax payable on buildings, but this kind of tax is not significant.

Subsidies

The most important financial means to encourage monument protection is the subsidy paid by the State via the National Board for Monuments. In 1993 the Board spent 400 million forints of its annual budget of 900 million forints (approximately $8 million U.S.) on financing or assisting restoration projects. This sum is no more than 5 to 7 percent of the annual national expenditure on the upkeep of monuments. Some local governments have preservation support budgets, too, but the decisive part of the costs has to be borne by the owners. Today,

- 10 to 20 percent of the monuments are owned by the State,
- 20 to 30 percent by local governments,
- 30 to 35 percent by churches and
- 25 to 30 percent by private individuals and companies.

Because of privatization, the number of church and private properties will surely increase during the next years.

Need for
legislative
review

Even after the amendments of 1991-1992, the present legislation is only partly successful in meeting the requirements

- of the new social and economic system and
- of the monument protection itself.

169

Hungary needs a true preservation law again. The duties undertaken in international conventions also require the renewal of legislation. (Hungary signed the Hague Convention in 1957, the UNESCO World Heritage Convention in 1985, and the Granada Convention of the Council of Europe in 1991.)

Process of review

In the fall of 1986, a working group began a general survey of the state of Hungarian monuments and the preparation of a future strategy for preservation. In May of 1989, the responsible committee of the Parliament of that time discussed the developed version of this report. By November of the same year, the Ministry prepared the outline of the new preservation law, but then the issue of the law was temporarily taken off the agenda. A few ideas from that outline have been built into the amendments of the existing laws of 1991-1992. Later on, the drafting resumed, and a draft bill was prepared in 1992-1993, but the bill has not been submitted yet to Parliament.

Simultaneous legislative changes

The preparation of the new Historic Preservation Act is being done in parallel with the new laws on environment protection, nature conservation and landscape protection, regional development and built environment. The latter is going to replace the Building Act of 1964 and is destined to regulate the formation, maintenance and protection of the built environment in general. Related to the general law on built environment, the Historic Preservation Act should include the special rules of protection of particular pieces of architectural heritage.

Current proposal

The starting point of the draft bill on monuments is that monuments are the common cultural heritage of the whole nation. The law would address

- monuments (i.e., protected buildings, which would be in one category instead of the present three),
- conservation areas, and
- protected environments registered on the basis of exact criteria.

Proposed duties

The draft has clearly defined the duties of the State, the local governments and the owners. The owners have to maintain the monuments, and their rights of disposal would be restricted in the name of the public interest. The law would also impose other duties on the owners and assure wide-scale means of State control. A certain number of outstanding monuments (100 to 300) would remain inalienable State properties by law.

Proposed planning for various properties

The objectives of protection and rehabilitation of historic districts would be co-ordinated with town planning and town development. A separate chapter would deal with the protection of

- historic gardens,

- cemeteries, and
- underground remains of built structures.

Another chapter would treat demands concerning culture, education and research in connection with monument protection.

Proposed
economic
aspects

The chapter on financial principles addresses

- the tax system,
- customs,
- credit policy, and
- the demand for a preservation fund.

The draft also deals with

- penalties,
- the possibilities of expropriation and first refusal, and
- protective measures in case of extraordinary occurrences.

Strategic
observations

Essential
re-orientation

The draft has several advanced elements. We need restrictive rules, too; but on the other hand, one negative feature is that the present (maybe not the final) draft relies upon the dominating role of the State against the citizens and the citizens' groups. It is a matter of course that the monuments cannot be protected against the people but together with them, relying upon the civil initiatives and taking into consideration the individual and collective interests, too.

Financial
problems

Another vulnerable point is that the financial conditions or objectives can be left out of consideration by the financial legislation, or fulfilled only in a symbolic way.

Higher
legal authority

This leads to the question of whether it would not be right to include the right to a proper human environment (wholesome both from physical and intellectual points of view) in higher-level "framework legislation on the environment" or, more importantly, in the Constitution itself, together with the basic requirements and means of realization.

Legislative Challenges and Ambitions in Ukraine

*Leonid Prybeha**

Comparative
analysis

Ukraine is interested in the mechanisms and approaches used by other countries, in the legislative area, for historic preservation. These allow Ukrainians to develop laws and identify shortcomings in Ukraine's historic preservation legislation. At present, there are several legislative variants in connection with historic monuments. Unfortunately, not all are effective in the new economic and social circumstances.

Changes in
function

The greatest problem, at present, is the economic aspect of historic preservation, including questions relating to privatization of land that has historical and cultural significance (archaeological zones, large ensembles, fortresses, defence complexes, etc.). This entire issue is within the scope of present preservation efforts. For example, in many Ukrainian cities, there are historic structures that, as a result of privatization, may be given new functions, either pursuant to the laws that regulate and implement this privatization process or because of problems that arise during the restoration of their interiors. As a result, only an exterior or outer shell of the original structure is retained. Historic monuments should be treated like objects of exceptional artistic or architectural merit, i.e., as works of art and also as historical documents. It is important to clarify the definition of what should be preserved and the legislative means to pursue those ends.

Objectives

Historic preservation in Ukraine is not as threatened as in some other countries by a process of demolition of monuments. With independence, Ukraine has been working on compiling its historic and cultural monuments into a national register. The former ideology limited manifestations of national traditions, whether

* Leonid Prybeha is Professor of Architecture at the Academy of Arts of Kiev and President of ICOMOS-Ukraine.

in culture or in the preservation of monuments, so Ukraine must now address the task of including in the register those monuments that embody the historical epochs of national history in order to truthfully portray the historical processes that took place on Ukrainian territory.

The challenging legal context

Ukraine has embarked on a search to find new approaches in the field of historic preservation. It is actively working on the development of preservation legislation that would put in place a gradual, step-by-step, effective strategy for the privatization of individual structures. This is likely to be complex, because many of the historical and cultural monuments, relics and museum artifacts will remain in the public sector. However, the structures that make up the fabric of historic towns will be privatized according to laws that regulate the use of these structures.

Legislative trategy

The whole range of necessary preservation legislation is still in its formative stages. The problem is the necessity of creating an entire system of laws that would support preservation efforts, for instance, land law. In the Ukrainian land code, there should be provisions concerning land of historical and cultural significance, its status and use. Without this kind of definition, the restoration work may actually damage the cultural component or objects of archaeological importance of the landscape, i.e., elements that contribute to the significance of the monument.

Strengths and weaknesses

In Ukraine, the "infrastructure" of researching and analyzing historic monuments has survived, i.e., the process that directs the development of project documentation and documenting the progress of restoration work. However, the financing required for these restoration efforts is very limited. Economics does not allow this work to proceed, and Ukraine needs funds to sustain this infrastructure.

Proper access to expertise

There is the problem of licensing restoration firms. Frequently, unqualified people have a negative effect on the quality of the restoration process. This is ironic, because Ukraine does indeed have a reasonable supply of experts who fully understand what is involved in the preservation of historic monuments and advanced methodologies of restoration.

These professionals are at the basis of Ukrainian optimism about preserving all of this country's monuments, not only national shrines, but those of interest to the international community. In this way, historic preservation will help Ukraine become a better part of the European and global community.

The Fragility of Laws in a War Zone

Jadran Antolović*

Historic
background

In an ideal world, the following presentation would focus on the evolution of legislation for the protection of historic buildings in Croatia. This legal tradition had its roots in the statutes of Korkula (1254), Dubrovnik (1272) and Split (1312). After application of the Vatican's *Lex Pacca* (1820), this process accelerated. As of today, the independent Republic of Croatia has new legislation entitled the Law on the Protection of Cultural Monuments; this was drafted with the assistance of experts sent by the Council of Europe, and its primary instrument is the Institute for the Protection of Cultural Monuments in Zagreb. However, there is a series of laws that are directly on point (e.g., Special Decree on the Uniform Activity of the Service for the Protection of Cultural Monuments). A comprehensive synopsis of the Croatian legislative picture is available from the Institute[§].

Current reality

However, unlike the situation in certain other countries of Central Europe (where the situation of historic buildings is difficult enough), war damage to the Croatian cultural heritage turned the already difficult condition into a dramatic one. The deficiencies of the legal system are observed even at the international level, since the country was unable to protect its treasures or stop vandalism. The following discussion therefore focuses on a single topic: the overriding problem of wartime.

Rule of law?

In theory, the basic precondition for implementing the protection of cultural monuments is the existence of corresponding laws. It would seem logical to think that a better quality of law would ensure better (and more efficient) protection of cultural properties. However, this is not the case, since a good law is not the only precondition of a good cultural properties protection

---

* Jadran Antolović is a lawyer and General Secretary of the Croatian Institute for Protection of Cultural Monuments (under the Croatian Ministry of Culture) in Zagreb.
§ The author is referring to an excellent summary that he wrote and that is printed in English under the name *Cultural Monuments' Legal Protection of the Republic of Croatia*. It is available in English from the Institute for Protection of Cultural Monuments, Ilica 44, 41000 Zagreb, Croatia.

175

Dubrovnik's status as a heritage city recognized under the UNESCO World Heritage Convention did not stop it from being shelled. Comparable damage is to be seen among countless historic buildings throughout the region. (Giorgio Croci)

system. The situation is reminiscent of 1944 when, in classic understatement, the Croatian conservator Andela Horvat wrote that "there are laws which may preserve monuments in the country, prevent their demolition, damage, and bad restoration — and even punish offences, if these are the result of someone's neglect or intentional act. This may all be considered in theory, but not yet in practice, since art conservation in Croatia cannot be properly implemented for the time being, because of the lack of trained people — and of the difficult circumstances under which we are living."

Hague Convention

Most notably, this conference has made several references to the Hague Convention of 1954. This is the Convention on the Protection of Cultural Property in the Event of Armed Conflict and is the successor to a long series of treaties on this subject. Under the convention, a "distinctive emblem" would be used to identify important properties for which every effort at protection should be used during armed conflict. Croatia posted these emblems on its important monuments, in the same way that the other countries mark their own important monuments. This is where Croatia learned some hard lessons for the international community.

Reverse effect

At the time that the Convention was drafted, it was not generally expected that the distinctive emblems of the Hague Con-

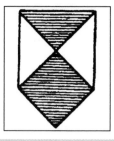

This shield is the "distinctive emblem" for important cultural property which is *intended* for protection under the Hague Convention. [The Hague Convention of 1954 is, in several key respects, merely a successor to another convention (also signed at the Hague and called Hague IV) entitled *Convention on Laws and Customs of War on Land* (1907); Art. 56 of the 1907 convention states that "all seizure of, destruction or wilful damage done to...historic monuments ... is forbidden." (This was in turn the direct successor to Art. 56 of a previous convention called Hague II of 1899.) These principles, of which the Hague Convention of 1954 is the latest articulation, were also enforced at the Nuremburg Trials. The destruction of "cultural monuments" was part of the indictment (s. 8) read at the trials as being "contrary to international conventions...the laws and customs of war, the general principles of criminal law...the internal penal laws of the countries in which such crimes are committed (etc.)." The principal defendant, pertaining to policies of systematic destruction and looting of heritage property, was the Nazi official Alfred Rosenberg; for these and other offences against humanity, Rosenberg was convicted, sentenced and hanged. *Ed.*]

vention would be used as the equivalent of a bull's eye for target practice by troops who had consciously and deliberately set out to destroy the cultural patrimony of another population.

The problem is obvious, particularly where there is no viable system of enforcement or punishment affecting offenders.

Amendment   For this reason, the Hague Convention must be rethought. It is essential that the international community explore this subject, in order to identify a new and better way to ensure the treaty protection of such properties.

Croatia has proposed a series of amendments to the Hague Convention. Croatia's concerns with the convention relate to the following examples:

- Article 4(2) concerning protection;
- Article 15 (which should have impeded the expulsion of the conservation personnel);

- Articles 18 and 19, which have also proven problematic, because although the Convention applies to "international" armed conflict, the situation can become confused if one of the belligerents claims that the dispute is "domestic" and hence the Convention never applied in the first place.

Information

A more detailed description of Croatia's recommendations concerning the Convention is available from the Institute, under the title *Report on the Implementation of the Convention on the Protection of Cultural Property in the Event of War Conflict.*

Part VII:

Conclusion

The Challenges Ahead

*Jaroslav Liptay**

The
challenge
of
complacency

It has now been many years since President John F. Kennedy told the American people, "Ask not what your country can do for you, but rather what you can do for your country." By contrast, Central Europe is in a more difficult position, although some personalities there speak to the citizens in similar terms. Many seem all too willing to listen to promises, even exceeding what people asked for. Unfortunately, that has been the level of political debate. Citizens lived for over forty years during a time when all of Central Europe's problems were "solved" by the State, and citizens always knew what awaited them for the next five years. There are still many citizens who would prefer the State to solve their problems rather than take responsibility for themselves. Unfortunately, it is sometimes as hazardous to gain freedom as to lose it.

The challenge of value

This is part of the general backdrop to life in Central Europe. But there are other problems: one of the most difficult is the valuation of Central Europe's cultural heritage. Since coming to the conclusion that we "cannot put a price" on cultural heritage because it is "priceless," perhaps we cannot insure any cultural heritage component because insurance cannot address and cover priceless values. It is globally recognized that many countries must awake to a better accounting system. In a country like Slovakia, that statement applies twofold, because this country never had an accounting system that would let us value cultural properties; there was a false system that simply ignored these values. The values were fictitious (on paper), and the values were not counted in currency. Today, owners — including the State and local governments — must be conscious of how valuable these properties really are. Conservation officials are finally entitled to consider the realistic value of the use of these properties, in order to look successfully to preserving them.

Appraisal

---

* Jaroslav Liptay is an architect at the Slovak Institute for Monuments. While at the Slovak Ministry of Culture, he headed legislative policy for heritage buildings.

The dilemma
of the State

To provide a real-life look at the effects of these issues, the Smolenice Castle Conference is being followed by a demonstration sites visit, which includes Slovakia's three areas on the World Heritage List. For example, participants will see graphic evidence that the law that Slovakia has been working on recently did not move very far because there has been no settlement of the issue of the legal responsibility of owners, under the current law, in contrast to the proposed preservation law. Monuments owned by private persons, as well as churches, tend to be in better physical condition than monuments owned by the State and local governments. State ownership is becoming the poorest ownership category and the monuments in State ownership in Spiš and Banská Štiavnica are in the worst condition of the monuments to be seen.

Key
observation

It is not realistic to expect that the same State, which lacks the money to care for its own properties, will be able to grant funds to other owners.

This is the biggest problem in a country like Slovakia, but perhaps if we look for a solution through the tax system, things will slowly improve as we search for these needed solutions.

Many countries (not only in Central Europe) are living in an unbelievable time of experimentation. They are trying to move into a market system (and improve manufacturing relationships for the market system), yet these same manufacturing facilities are still largely State-owned; quite candidly, many are still under the old socialistic system, which continues in operation but cannot do so indefinitely. It is not only a political problem, but also an economic problem.

The importance
of legal context

A country like Slovakia cannot progress into the market system unless it recognizes a two-pronged reality:

- a country must create good legislation of general application,
- only then can it create good legislation specifically for historic preservation.

There is also the added problem that some people in Parliament are anxious to abolish existing laws — without reflecting on the new laws to put in their place. This type of problem haunts a country when some parliamentarians have not yet learned how to act responsibly.

The challenge
of an
unpredictable
economy

This has consequences for the economy. For example, yesterday's evening news in Slovakia announced that the government was expected to raise the taxes in one sector — but raised them in another sector instead, opening a new tax break. Economists realize that this flip-flop must have consequences for our economy. Furthermore, it is difficult to measure whether the consumer is capable of paying these higher taxes; citizens buy goods daily, but with the higher consumer taxes, they may buy less than what was expected. This whole process is obviously not in equilibrium. This pushes the country towards other legislative and economic laws, made worse by our unstable economic and political situation.

Preaching to the unconverted

I am not a lawyer, but an architect. I am not an expert on taxes or on finance, and I don't try to be, but it is essential for these experts to become involved. Not long ago, the Slovak Ministry of Culture had a formal meeting with the Ministry of Finance and asked for consideration of tax benefits related to historic buildings. The answer was a flat "No!" There is now a new government, and obviously there will be new attempts to persuade tax officials of the good sense of such measures, but it is a shame that officials with this expertise are so absent from discussions such as the ones undertaken here, where they could share in these ideas.

There are further problems — for example, the division of responsibility between the State and local administrations.

Analogy of the key

In conclusion, I offer one analogy from this very location. On Monday, the Smolenice Castle tower was not open for anyone to see the magnificent view — Tuesday the tower was open, but it was too foggy to see anything. All that was required was to use the right key for the door on the correct day. Similarly, the bottom line for all of our problems is to find the right key and use it at the right time. We only need to find the right key and method.

Valedictory

I am not speaking officially for the Ministry, and I am not officially charged with conveying an official message from the Ministry. I personally thank the foreign lecturers who have contributed to this discussion; I am sure that Slovakia and other countries will try to make maximum use of their information in creating new legislation. The preparation of new laws depends on a number of factors, many of which have nothing to do with the preservation of monuments — but the final result will be similar to my example of the tower, the key and the weather. We must carry forth in our work with a maximum of logic, understanding and common sense. We are on our way, and we have some trials before us which we must go through. I hope that if I meet you again in the near future, I will be able to state that we have made progress.

Summary

*Marc Denhez**

Goals of this
Conference

In his conference theses, Mr. Kilián invited the participants to address objectives and priorities.

Defining objectives is not too difficult — the international community has already provided us with many examples of the objectives that it has recommended. In one sense, they can be summarized in a single phrase: the protection of buildings.

Overall strategy

Planning priorities is more difficult. At the international level, overall strategy has been provided by the international declarations, and I remind you that virtually every country in the world has officially adopted these international declarations.

When turning to tactics, these have also been recommended by the international community. In order, those topics are:

Review of topics

- Physical planning (described in methodical detail by Mr. Jeschke).
- Control of the public sector (described by Mr. Mayes, and in part by Mr. Croci).
- Encouragement of the public sector (not described in great detail in the existing international literature, and which can be discussed at another time).
- Control of the private sector (described by Mr. Dornic, Mr. Dennis, Ms. Miner, Mr. Lund, Mr. Croci and Mr. Rupp).
- Encouragement of the private sector (described by Mr. Dornic and Ms. Mead).
- Facilitation, which means citizens working with other citizens (with an excellent example described by Mr. Howard).

The question of relevance

However, there are profound concerns in places like Central Europe. Some people say that the international dimension is "interesting," and it is "nice to see the approaches of people with a different political, economic, cultural and social situation — but what does it have to do with me?

---

* Conference Rapporteur

- I have no money.
- I have no government support.

Therefore, the international materials have no true bearing on my situation."

Is inadequacy of resources insurmountable?

In response, the assistance that can be given by the international community cannot and should not be in "suitcases full of money" nor in the form of guidance resembling Moses parting the Red Sea. Ultimately, in no country did conservationists begin with such a lucky scenario. Every country on earth that has done things for its national heritage has started at zero.

The starting point: Law

Nor are all foreign experiences equally applicable; indeed, the introduction of certain foreign experiences is likely to cause some confusion. For example, if René Descartes had attended this conference, some people might now believe that instead of his "*cogito ergo sum*", he would have said, "I get sued, therefore I am." In some countries, regardless of how their programs start, their "reality" is tested only when there has been a lawsuit and the program has been approved by the courts. Only then do officials in those countries feel comfortable that the program truly works.

Conceptual challenges

This may be an extremely strange concept in places like Central Europe. Furthermore, the reason that this "testing" happens was explained in detail by Mr. Lund: there is an extremely delicate balance in any country, when the country starts from the initial premise that there is a system of private property rights, and it wishes also to have a system for the protection of the national heritage.

Balancing property rights

Acknowledging variety

No two countries on the earth have defined exactly the same balance. The best proof was Mr. Rupp's presentation on one single subject, namely that of the protection of accessories. The topic of accessories is proof that there is no single international formula, because even on this one very specific subject, there are almost as many formulas as there are countries.

It has also been pointed out that people (and countries) will make mistakes and learn from them.

Acknowledging other complexities

I offer one comment parenthetically. The writer André Malraux became, for a time, Minister of Culture for France; in this position, he prepared a new law on the protection of heritage property. If conservationists want to see a law that proceeds as René Descartes himself might have written it, they look at the Malraux law. It starts from general principles, and it proceeds, with unstoppable logic, to the creation of an entire complex system for the protection of property. This law is probably the most widely imitated law on the earth for the protection of cultural property. It works extremely well in a certain context.

Acknowledging differences of context

It would have been easy for presenters to come to a conference like this, give the telephone number of the Council of Europe, and say that if the audience wanted an "instant solution," it could ask the Council of Europe to send a copy of the Malraux law. However, there is a problem with that "instant solution": the Malraux law comes from a country that has a clear idea of property rights, although those property rights are not entrenched in its constitution; and the country has a relatively centralized system of authority.

On the other hand, as described by Dr. Kosová, the situation in places like Central Europe is entirely different; nobody knows yet exactly what property rights will look like or how much centralization is going to occur in governments in Central Europe. We do not even know how the building and construction laws are going to be drafted.

Being undeterred by obstacles

What are strategists supposed to do with a confusing situation like that? To find the answer, one should remember the point that Mr. Dennis raised: in the United States, it took almost ninety years to develop the system that exists today. The lesson is not that conservationists should wait for decades; on the contrary, the lesson is to look at what Mr. Dennis described next:

- There are over 6,000 historic districts in the United States today;
- that happened in a country where the governmental support system was not obvious, the ability to control private property was not obvious, and the economic forces — instead of being lined up in favour of the protection of the national heritage — were lined up against the national heritage (many times worse than the situation in places like Central Europe).

International message: Do the possible

The conclusion that one may draw from this is that a country does what it can. This is how other countries have developed the legislation that they have: like politics generally, this legislation is ultimately "the art of the possible."

Imagination over formulas

The final question is: what message was this conference intended to convey?

- It does not provide an instant magic formula for the creation of legislation to protect heritage.
- It does not provide a magic formula for the printing of money.
- What it is intended to convey is a sense that conservationists

in places like Central Europe are now in a position to start thinking about creating their own formulas themselves.

The first step, as Mrs. Saaby pointed out, is to look at the guidance from the international community, but then a country must go further.

Building on public support

Ms. Jenčová* asked the question: how does the conservation community make progress in a situation where it cannot rely upon government support? In response (and in any event, as Mr. Lund pointed out), the effectiveness of legislation would depend on public opinion anyway. Conservation cannot function effectively in a legislative system independently of public opinion. The ideal, of course (to use Ms. Mead's expression), is to develop "consensus-based planning." But who is going to lead the consensus? Who is going to take the first steps to make sure that national consensus can be reached?

Government is no longer the "leader"

For decades, in places like Central Europe, the answer to that question was "easy": leadership would come from the government. However, as Mr. Liptay pointed out, some people in the government (or at least in the Slovak Ministry of Finance) have not exactly been the best of friends; and as Mr. Mayes pointed out, in the area of heritage the government is often the largest threat.

Developing leadership

Ultimately, what saved the day in the United States (as Mr. Dennis pointed out) was conferences. In other words, the question of leadership is inextricably linked to networks among the public.

To recap, let us return to the question of identifying the strategy and the tactics.

There was an explanation from various lawyers and other professionals about a wide variety of tools that are being used in other countries. These various tools were described by Mr. Dornic, Ms. Miner, Ms. Mead and Mr. Croci. What conclusion can be drawn from these presentations? Is the conclusion that it is better, for example, to have five people on the New York City Landmarks Commission or nine people or eleven people? Clearly not. That was not the purpose of these presentations.

Asking he right questions

Instead, the conclusion is that there are a number of questions that each country has to be asking about what that country is going to do. Ms. Miner started her presentation with five questions that should be asked about a given system. There is an old saying in the legal profession: if you know how to ask the

---

* Alžbeta Jenčová is an architect and advisor to restoration efforts in Banská Stiavnica, Slovakia.

right question, you already have 75 percent of your answer.

This is the message that this conference is intended to communicate. It is not the role of international presenters "to part the Red Sea" for you: it is your assignment to part the Red Sea for yourselves. Mrs. Saaby said that several tools will need to be used simultaneously, and Mr. Jeschke said that the ultimate goal is a "harmonization" of all those tools — but in the meantime, a country must be looking at tools that come from a wide variety of directions.

Law and the educational challenge

Certain points should be obvious from the presentations:

- the task will be multi-disciplinary, and perhaps even more importantly,
- the task is one of national education.

At least half the people at the Smolenice Castle conference were professional educators; they are now being called upon to undertake the largest "educational assignment" of their lives.

Mr. Rupp concluded by saying how beautiful it would be if we in the conservation movement could "unify our energies." Mr. Howard has given one example, among many, of ways to organize people, because (to use Mr. Petravich's phrase), "Monuments cannot be protected against the people but only with them." How does a country do that?

A process of evolution

In answer, Mr. Mayes made an extremely important comment: "You are going to make mistakes, but you will have the opportunity to correct those mistakes over time." And as Mr. Howard said, "You may only even be able to address one issue at a time. Build gradually year after year."

This brings the discussion back to the very first point that Mr. Kilián raised, about why this conference was taking place: to address the question of legislation and finance for heritage in the context of rebuilding democratic societies. I address this comment to members of the conservation community: on the subject of the national heritage, there is nobody else to lead public opinion except you.

Opportunity and creativity

Furthermore, as Mr. Dennis pointed out, if the Americans had asked ninety years ago how their own situation would evolve, nobody would have ever predicted what they have today. It is certainly not by the light of pure reason. It is the result of a whole series of events and of taking advantage of various opportunities as they presented themselves — but the opportunities are different in every country.

The message to the conservation community is clear. The

primary key, when talking about having "the right key, at the right time, at the right place," is going to be your own imagination and your own ability to deal creatively with the situations in your own countries. That is the challenge conveyed to you at this conference. The task starts with you, and the task starts today.

EPILOGUE

*Marc Denhez**

Conference
feedback

The comments concerning the subject-matter of the conference were expressed during the subsequent Demonstration Sites Visit, both individually (to the rapporteur) and collectively (at a "think-tank" session in Levoča).

Example of
preservation
plan

The visit covered Slovakia's three cultural sites on the World Heritage List, and included

- Vlkolínec, the hillside village whose nomination to the World Heritage List is likely to attract tourist attention, but whose bucolic character will be strictly preserved (despite expected tourist pressures);

Example of
unusual use

- Spiš Castle, the largest castle complex in Central Europe, which has been leased from time to time as a movie set;

Example of
privatization

- Spišská Kapitula, a village that had been entirely occupied by clerics in a previous era and that had now been returned to the Catholic Church under the State's restitution program;

Example of
prospective
tourism centre

- Levoča, whose tourist potential was not only rooted in its own important sites, but that was also expected to serve as a staging point for growing visits of the surrounding region; and

Another
example for
tourism

- Banská Štiavnica, which is also on the World Heritage List and which has been the focus of international attention to revitalize its economic potential.

In all of these cases, the strategy to attract international attention was relatively recent, and there was still much work to do.

Economic
imperatives

The general discussion in Levoča gravitated towards tourism. The discussion started from the premise that in countries like Slovakia, there were high expectations concerning the prospects for tourism development (e.g., in restored town centres), but this was tinged with a certain desperation because of the stagnation of the rest of the economy. In other words, the national heritage was being perceived as a future gold-mine not because national deci-

---

* Conference Rapporteur

The Demonstration Sites visit paid particular attention to several sites that Slovakia nominated to the World Heritage List, under the UNESCO World Heritage Convention. The village of Vlkolínec is a showpiece of traditional Slovak rural life (photos 1 and 2). Spi∑ Castle's international interest lay in a different area, namely its monumental proportions (photos 3 and 4). The area nominated with the castle includes the walled village of Spi∑ská Kapitula (photos 5 and 6), which has now been returned

sion makers had suddenly gained a sympathy for these resources, but rather by default.

Irony

The sense of desperation was compounded, at least among heritage officials, by the knowledge that they were expected to meet these rising expectations at precisely the same moment that their available funds were being reduced because of their countries' precarious budgetary situation. This left them in a most uncomfortable squeeze.

to the Roman Catholic church as part of Slovakia's restitution/privatization program. Banská ‡tiavnica (photo 7) bears both aesthetic significance and historic significance, particularly with reference to a variety of international technological firsts that occurred there. These sites, however, were also illustrative of both the assets and liabilities that may belong to heritage resources in many other countries. (Marc Denhez)

Trap

The logical response was obviously to seek "smarter" ways of accomplishing more with less. In the search for such measures, however, there was (not surprisingly) a temptation to seek shortcuts via formulaic solutions: "What is the ideal system for this or that?"

Backdrop

The Levoča think tank attempted to explore the tourism question further. The architectural quality of the central area of Levoča is so remarkable that the city is a likely magnet for tourism. In this respect, Levoča's case is similar to that of count-

St. Jacob's Church in Levoça, next to the historic Town Hall, contains the world's tallest Gothic altarpiece. Levoça was the site of a free-ranging discussion of the conference's conclusions among participants in the Demonstration Sites visit.

less other communities around the world where governments are giving increased attention to "cultural tourism," particularly as an instrument in the sometimes aggressive competition for foreign exchange.

The paradox of authenticity

The first question was: did Levoča actually want tourism? It was argued that the question was moot. A community has little choice or control over a prospective influx of tourists, but what it can do is to plan to handle this properly. For example, one of the strong elements that can attract tourists is a community's "untouched," "authentic" atmosphere; if the community attempts to over-exploit itself or turn itself (for the sake of tourists) into something that it is not, then it may defeat the very purpose of its efforts on the tourism front.

Similarly, such destinations must be capable of continuing to operate as living communities, as opposed to gigantic museum pieces. This objective presupposes substantial public participation in the planning process. As a corollary to the necessity to remain "living communities," the planning process must prevent local shops (which are necessary to sustain the local population) from being entirely displaced by tourist-oriented shops. Such displacement threatens a neighbourhood's ability to sustain its residential functions and character. Although the world is filled with horror stories of districts that had lost their normal character under the onslaught of tourists (Aigues-Mortes was cited as an example), this was considered more the result of a lack of foresight and preparedness rather than of an intrinsic dichotomy between the tourism interest and the normal character of the community.

Planning for
tourism

In short, it was not considered necessary that a community choose between two extremes, namely withering away economically or turning itself into a giant tourist traffic jam.

The challenge was to do intelligent physical planning that had clearly defined objectives. For example, the strategy may specifically include conservation of a residential character, or other uses (as the case may be). Two North Carolina towns were mentioned that had identified tourism as an objective, but that had also developed a specific strategy for attracting retirees.

Accounting for
distinctions

Another objective is to understand the kind of tourist being attracted, because different kinds of tourists will lead to different strategies. The reason is simple: different kinds of tourists have different demands, different spending patterns, etc.

Realism

Cultural tourism, in any event, should never be viewed as a panacea. Tourism jobs tend to be low-paying and are often seasonal. Furthermore, the primary economic benefits will not go to the historic area at all if this is not where the hotels and restaurants are located (money will gravitate towards the latter location): for example, tourism will not result in increased incomes within the village of Vlkolínec, but rather within the neighbouring towns.

Overriding
objective

Perhaps the most important conclusion reached at the Levoča session was that a tourist influx should be preceded by an intelligent community strategy, whose most important component is a commitment to the improvement of the quality of life of the residents.

"It can't be
done"

If the Levoča session could be described as relatively optimistic in its tone, the same was not entirely true of a similar discussion in Banská Stiavnica. That discussion included an inventory by local officials of the obstacles they had faced in their attempts to revitalize the historic community. The discussion appeared to demonstrate considerable success in identifying every conceivable hurdle, without any comparable results in identifying possible solutions.

In the opinion of one listener, this was the first "realistic" appraisal of the domestic situation for heritage property that she had heard during the entire conference and its follow-up.

The challenge
of pessimism

That unflattering assessment was reflective of a certain malaise that had been felt at Smolenice Castle. No symposium can profess to be all things to all people, and this conference was no exception. Simply put, a significant minority in the audience apparently held the view that the situation was so bleak that foreigners' descriptions of national strategies were (at best) glib or (at worst) irrelevant. "I have no money, and I have no influence," said one. "I don't have the ear of the government." "Anyone who talks to me about these national strategies simply doesn't understand our situation," said a heritage administrator.

This undercurrent of defeatism, though hardly unanimous, was nevertheless sufficiently widespread to remind other conference participants of the urgency of follow-up. In particular, four specific tactics were discussed by various participants among themselves, to respond directly to this concern.

Tactics for
follow-up

- **Target more lawyers, tax officials and "mainstream politicians":** The audience at Smolenice had been overwhelmingly weighted towards heritage administrators, but the next such meeting must attempt to co-opt more active participation among the very professionals who would be rewriting legal, financial and fiscal rules.

- **Include more short-term goals in the presentations:** The Smolenice conference had focused overwhelmingly on strategies and tactics for the mid-term and long-term (with typical lead times of three years and up), but professionals in many countries also want to see short-term goals (even under six months), which, although modest, can build confidence for the long road ahead.

- **Beware of "formula" solutions:** In many countries undergoing systemic change, there is a temptation to jump to the conclusion that since previous governmental formulas were "wrong," the country can make up for lost time by merely copying a different formula that is "right," as if systemic change were like a magic incantation. In reality, legal systems are the tip of a social iceberg, and although well-planned legislation can have significant domino effects, legal strategists at conferences such as these nevertheless have a duty to warn their audiences that the keys to social change cannot be learned by rote, nor can they rely upon formulas alone. Expectations of audiences must be linked to the social forces that the conservation community can mobilize and to the long-term effort that they can predict.

- **Emphasize advocacy skills:** In many countries, supporters of heritage have never had experience in playing an advocacy role in the development of legal, financial and fiscal rules and practices. Now that the socio-economic order has changed in many of these countries, they will need to learn state-of-the-art techniques of effective and discreet lobbying. The same applies for building public support; that public support is not only a worthy goal in itself, but must also be highly visible (for political purposes).

The above tactics were all considered to be worthy components for any follow-up conferences to be held on the subject.

Index

Other Architecture Books from Dundurn Press ...

The Heritage Strategy Planning Handbook
by Marc Denhez

A companion volume to *Legal and Financial Aspects of Architectural Conservation,* this book suggests strategies for the conservation and revitalization of buildings and districts. *The Heritage Strategy Planning Handbook* summarizes the five major legislative approaches, the treaties, and international declarations, outlining how to deal with these properties.

ISBN 1-55002-283-0
72 pages, paperback, $8.99 (US$8.00)

The Canadian Home: From Cave to Electronic Cocoon
by Marc Denhez

Would you want to live in a factory-molded cube made of plastic, asbestos, and UFFI? With an "H-bomb shelter" and nuclear furnace underneath? Or a house designed by God to harmonize with the cosmic Muzak?

The Canadian Home is a look at how Canadian housing came to be, from primeval origins to the R-2000 house and speculation about habitation in space.

ISBN 1-55002-202-4
350 pages, hardcover, $39.99 (US$35.25)

Dundurn Press books are distributed by University of Toronto Press. To order these or any other Dundurn books, please call 1(800)565-9523.

The Canadian Master Architects Series
from Dundurn Press

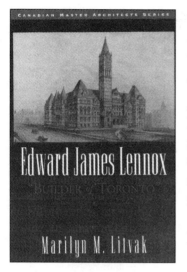

Edward James Lennox: Builder of Toronto
by Marilyn M. Litvak

The first book in the Canadian Master Architects Series, this volume analyzes the life and work of a man who left an indelible mark on the architecture of Toronto. From Old City Hall to Casa Loma, Lennox designed some of the most famous buildings in the city and the country.

ISBN 1-55002-204-0
124 pages, paperback, $19.99

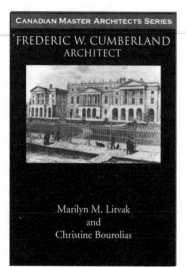

Frederic W. Cumberland
by Marilyn M. Litvak and Christine Bourolias

Like Lennox, F. W. Cumberland helped to build some of Toronto's most memorable structures. Cumberland's work included University College, St. James' Cathedral, and the central section of Osgoode Hall.

ISBN 1-55002-301-2
124 pages, paperback, $19.99

Dundurn Press books are distributed by University of Toronto Press. To order these or any other Dundurn books, please call 1(800)565-9523.